The Unwritten Text

The Unwritten Text

The Unwritten Text:
The Indigenous African Christian Women's Movement in Zimbabwe

Tumani Mutasa Nyajeka

Africa University Press

Mutare, Zimbabwe

Cover design: Shawn Marie Lancaster
Photo for cover art: Adlene Kufarimai and the Reverend Tiwirai Kufarimai

ISBN 0-9786343-0-6

Manufactured in the United States of America

To Panganayi, J. Mutasa, my father, who loved learning, religion, and dance.

And to my aunts, who died in the struggle to be human.

Contents

Acknowledgments

I WISH TO EXPRESS MY PROFOUND GRATITUDE TO DR. ROSEMARY RADFORD Ruether, my advisor, who, like *Nzou* the Elephant, gracefully guided and supported my work, to Professor John H.O. Hunwick of Northwestern University, and to Professor Jacquelyn Grant, a mentor and colleague. Thanks also to Dr. Edward P. Wimberly—*Humba*—vice president for academic services/provost of the Interdenominational Theological Center, and Dr. Anne Streaty Wimberly—*Shava*—whose devotion to the church and the community is unwavering.

To Ben, my companion, our children, Rungano, Nhanda, Zambuko, and all the children of the world; my late mother-in-law, Phoebe Chirewa, and my mother, Lois Nyakatawa, Rukwadzano women whose lives are a testimony of courage and conviction.

To my editor, Hendrik Pieterse, whose work and mine point to the beauty of the past, the present, and the future of us as children of Africa. Finally, to James H. Salley, associate vice-chancellor for institutional advancement for Africa University, and Eben K. Nhiwatiwa, bishop of the Zimbabwe episcopal area—two men whose commitment to the church and the academy is visionary.

Foreword

AT THE APRIL 26, 2006, ANNUAL COPHER LECTURES AT INTERDENOMINATIONAL Theological Center (ITC), the focus was on the "Jesus' Possession Paradox: Its Genesis in the Making of the Black Church Self-Worth Consciousness." The lecturer, ITC faculty member Riggins Earl, focused his lecture on the influence of white Christianity on the African-American slave understanding of Jesus. The central question was whether our African-American Christian understanding of Jesus and spirit possession was influenced more by our African origins, by white Christianity, or by a combination of these two influences. One of the respondents to the lecture, obviously trying to plow new ground for understanding the genesis of interpretations of Jesus and cultural influences, pointed out the need for studies carried out in places in Africa where African Christians appropriated the Christian faith without the supervision and oversight of white Christians and missionaries. The individual spoke as if such a project had yet to be undertaken. Afterward, I told one of the respondents to the lecture that this research had already been done by Tumani Nyajeka, a member of our faculty at ITC!

Tumani skillfully tells the story of how native Zimbabwean women encountered the incarnated Christ as they read the Scriptures and how this encounter transformed their lives and their personal identities. She shows how this transformation happened without the tutoring and mentoring relationships with white missionaries.

An E. Stanley Jones Associate Professor of Evangelism, Tumani occupies the Cornelius and Dorothye Henderson Chair at Gammon Theological Seminary/ITC. She received this chair during my tenure as academic dean. Her appointment was the culmination of a long pilgrimage. I will chronicle briefly the steps in the pilgrimage, since it sheds more light on the contents of this magnificent book.

I first encountered Tumani when she was a candidate for the Ph.D. degree from a joint-degree program between Garrett-Evangelical

Theological Seminary and Northwestern University. I happened to be a faculty member at Garrett-Evangelical at that time. She and I never thought that we might be teaching colleagues on the same theological faculty one day, but this happened in the middle of the 1990s, at ITC. Thus I met Tumani for the second time, this time as a colleague in the same academic department.

One of the program directors at the United Methodist Board of Global Ministries asked Tumani and me to serve as consultants to a group of Africans in the Diaspora in the United States. Our task was to address the needs of these Africans as well as to address the many needs of those in Africa. We discovered that those of us in the Diaspora and those in Africa had one thing in common: All of us had been impacted by the modern phenomenon of the loss of village life and village functioning. We concluded that one of the major tasks for Africans both in the Diaspora and in Africa was to restore and recover village functioning. Consequently, we began to talk about what this would look like for those of us who are Christian.

In the process, Tumani began to talk about African cultural traditions that were essential for our agenda of recreating the village. She spoke of an organization of indigenous African women who creatively and imaginatively began a woman's movement by integrating the essence of the Christian faith with indigenous cultural practices. From her observations, we realized that the foundation of our re-village construction should begin with our Christian faith and then be integrated with those cultural traditions compatible with it.

We discovered that, in addition to the women's movement, the Zimbabwe Annual Conference used the intergenerational small-group and the cell-group concepts to recover village life. The Bible, preaching, teaching, and stewardship practices were taught in an intergenerational way. The end result was that small-village communities were established in the urban environment. We put some conceptual flesh on the intergenerational village model, and we began to do workshops on the model.

When the Foundation for Evangelism awarded ITC and Gammon Theological Seminary money for a chair in evangelism, Tumani's name surfaced; and after a national search she was appointed to this chair. At the time of her appointment, few of us recognized the cutting-edge nature of her research. Now, however, is the appropriate time for this book to be made public. *The Unwritten Text* affirms that it is possible for the Bible to reveal the essential message of the Christian faith to people as they interpret it and translate it within their own cultural context and location. The significance of this work is that the Christian message transcends all cultural entrapments, and people from different cultures can be grasped by the message and can appropriate its essence as they encounter Christ through reading and translating the Bible for themselves. This grasping and appropriating the essential message of Scripture can take place without the mentoring and tutoring from colonial-minded missionaries.

Some of us scholars worry about local communities translating and interpreting Scripture without being tutored. We are often worried about the distortions and ideological agendas of those who are untutored or academically untrained. Tumani Nyajeka's work shows that a group of women engaged in discerning the meaning of the faith through Bible reading can catch the central message of Scripture without distorting it. This central message is that the kingdom of God is present and people are invited to join with God in bringing the kingdom on earth. It is possible for people meeting in small groups to study the Bible to discern and appropriate this message in ways that make daily living meaningful and purposeful.

The message the reader will take away from this wonderful work is that authentic Christianity can emerge from indigenous communities whether or not they have been exposed to colonial missionaries or to those who seek to use Scripture to serve oppression. While distortions do take place, the disclosing and revelatory power of Scripture continually seeks to overthrow distortions in order that authentic faith can develop. Furthermore, Scripture helps small groups of people to appropriate its message and express it through local, indigenous cultural traditions.

—Edward P. Wimberly

Preface

CRITICISM THAT MISSIONARY CHRISTIANITY IMPORTED THE COLONIAL mindset into its work in Africa has been well documented. In this book, I show how a group of indigenous African women took the essence of the Christian faith—a significant relationship with God through Jesus Christ—and fashioned and translated it into the African communal, holistic, and relational orientation to the world. I demonstrate how indigenous people correlated the essence of Christianity with their indigenous, or original, African worldview and developed an African Christianity, much as African Americans did in the context of the United States.

I point out that colonial Christianity was patriarchal, paternalistic, racist, and culturally alienating. Yet, within it, African women discerned the essence of the Christian message and began to take that message into their daily lives. The women in their church organization, Rukwadzano, fashioned faith practices similar to those found in the early church and used its communal, holistic, and relational understanding of the world to develop a faith relevant to the lives of African people.

The book also demonstrates the essential role of women in the preservation of relational, communal, and holistic values in a cultural orientation where nurturing and caring values are not sanctioned. The fact is, the essence of Christianity can be discerned even when the original intent of some missionaries was to westernize Africans.

Contemporary liberal Christianity promotes the idea that evangelical Christianity is biblically oriented in a way that is negative. Evangelical Christianity, the charge goes, is otherworldly, politically conservative, rejects those who are different, and is irrelevant for living life in this modern age. In fact, some dismiss an evangelistic African orientation as a creation of colonial Christianity and therefore discount its significance. However, I show that it is possible for

African Christians to embrace a biblically based faith centered on a relationship with God through Jesus Christ and not be disengaged from the world, politically conservative, or dismissive of those who are different. Indeed, in these pages, I tell the story of a women's organization that, through the power of the gospel, reached out to the poor and needy to uplift them and give them a sense of meaning.

The book further addresses the collapse of the village in today's world and the desperate need to recover some of its functions. Small groups, I argue, are essential for living meaningfully in a twenty-first-century world that privileges individualism and makes human worth a commodity to be bought and sold.

The Unwritten Text is written for clergy, theological students, and lay people who are interested in the relationship between missiology and evangelism—in how the gospel can be made relevant by a group of indigenous people. In analyzing the material and writing the book, I used an indigenous approach to the gospel in contradistinction to a colonial approach to "foreign missions." The colonial approach imports Western culture and all of its trappings, seeking to transport its cultural baggage along with the gospel. By contrast, an indigenous approach is a *post-colonial* orientation, where the gospel takes seriously the local cultural context and is relevant to the people who must appropriate the meaning of Christianity for themselves. Thus, this book is about how a group of African women took the essence of the Christian gospel and made it speak to their own religious, spiritual, economic, social, cultural, and gender-specific context.

The book will also be of interest to those who are interested in evangelism. The book views evangelism as the witnessing by word and deed to the good news of God's reign incarnated in Jesus Christ, good news that is for every culture and context. Evangelism is empowered by the Holy Spirit; and the Spirit inspires and empowers those persons and communities to make the gospel relevant to their own local contexts.

The Unwritten Text will also be of help to those who are interested in how local groups of people in Africa allow the Bible to speak to their own local situation despite efforts to shape the gospel message in ways irrelevant to the local cultural context. I show how a local group of African women allowed the Bible to shape and form their lives despite other intentions by Western missionaries.

Finally, the book may be of relevance to historians and others who are interested in pre-colonial Zimbabwe and the role women played in traditional African culture. African women are portrayed as those who are not only guardians and stewards of relational values but also agents making the gospel relevant to the indigenous culture in Zimbabwe.

My hope in writing *The Unwritten Text* is that readers will be able to decipher the essence of the Christian gospel from the cultural trappings that often accompany many mission and evangelistic efforts. It emphasizes how God establishes God's own reign and rule in diverse cultures and works through local indigenous people. God draws local people into this process and empowers local groups of people to resist efforts to distort God's evangelizing effort. The process of evangelization must become a local effort without the domination of outside groups. The pages that follow chronicle just such an effort—a story of a small women's group establishing an authentic response to the gospel of Jesus Christ within a local non-western culture.

Introduction

Until 1980, the largest body of organized women in Zimbabwe was Rukwadzano, a church women's organization. Studies on women's organizations in a politically free Zimbabwe are in their initial stages. Historically, Rukwadzanos have been thought of as predominantly attracting the semiliterate, urban, and rural women members of the church. This picture began changing near the end of the 1980s. Suddenly, these organizations experienced an infusion of young members, educated in Western countries. They were professional women, including medical doctors, teachers, and professors.[1] This new and professional interest in the Rukwadzanos sparked a great deal of interest and began to pique my own curiosity.

As the first woman to be ordained an elder (in 1980, the year in which Zimbabwe gained independence) in the Zimbabwe Annual Conference of The United Methodist Church, I have always been interested in the role religion plays in the lives of Zimbabwean women. Today, these women's organizations are experiencing rapid growth, with membership representing a cross section of Zimbabwean women. To satisfy my curiosity about such rapid growth as well as to provide a systematic statement for those who may want to examine the growth and development of this movement, I have set out to provide in these pages a historical account of this development.

In telling the story of the Rukwadzanos, I do more than provide a historical account, however. I am also witnessing to an unfolding story of God's salvation drama encountering a group of African women who almost immediately saw the relevance of the Christian gospel for their own predicament of living in colonial culture. This account takes seriously the indigenous women's participation in the development of the women's organization, and my telling is influenced by the fact that my mother has been a member of Rukwadzano of the Methodist Episcopal Church for nearly fifty years.

Historical Accounts of the Development of Rukwadzano

There are two accounts of the development of the Rukwadzanos and Manyanos, both southern African women's organizations. The more widely accepted account has been that these organizations are citadels of Western mission-church activity functioning as mediums of a systemic oppression of women by the Western church. Generally, women in these organizations have been portrayed as victims of both a Christian effort to domesticate and an oppressive traditional past. Most scholars associate these women with prayer and a cult of motherhood in which they are said to wail incessantly, penitently asking for God to preserve their daughter's virginity.[2] This view is narrow, misleading, and inaccurate, because it uses a non-historical method of study and ignores certain important factors. For example, it overlooks the pre-colonial history of women in the Rukwadzano and Manyanos of southern African societies[3] and ignores the history of the African women's experience of racism, colonialism, and domination.[4]

An alternative account holds that these women's organizations represent an authentic African women's creative response to a new religion encountered in the harsh and oppressive context of colonial domination. Proponents of this view argue that southern African church-women's organizations ought to be studied as part of the independence movement within African Christianity during the colonial era.[5]

In examining the beginnings and founding of Rukwadzano at Old Mutare, Mutare, Zimbabwe, I focus primarily on the latter view. Founded in 1898 and situated in the Nyangani mountains, about ten miles north of the city of Mutare, Old Mutare was the first mission site of the Methodist Episcopal Church. Mutare is located east of Harare near the border between Zimbabwe and Mozambique. The Old Mutare site was settled by the British South Africa Company around 1897, soon after it had prevailed against the Portuguese competition from the east and the Mutasa, who governed the territory.[6] After a brief stay, the company relocated its settlement to the site of the present-day city of Mutare. In a meeting with Cecil Rhodes in London, Bishop Joseph C. Hartzell of the Methodist Episcopal

Church was given the land and property at the Old Mutare site.[7]

A historical study of the beginnings of Rukwadzano is critical to the understanding of the basic beliefs and structure that informed and shaped the organization's convictions about life. The process entails identifying and analyzing sources from which the organization drew its fundamental convictions and beliefs about life and the world. Rukwadzano was founded at a Protestant Christian mission center in a colonial context by women from two cultural heritages. The first grouping was comprised of young Manyika/Shona women who came to the mission to learn and were taught by American Protestant women missionaries at Old Mutare. They were trained to become "Bible women" and also were groomed to marry aspiring young men training to become pastors or teachers at the mission school. Drawing on the Manyika worldview and colonial American Protestant Christianity, Manyika women, who were wives of pastors and teachers, started a movement in 1929. The movement was officially recognized by the Methodist Episcopal Church in 1938.

On the surface, this women's movement had a rigid exterior, resembling the religious orthodoxy and organizational structure of the Western missionary. At a more profound level, however, a deeper spiritual and organizational dynamic was at work. This dynamic became evident in the encounter of African women with the Bible, introduced by the Western missionaries, and the African traditional culture that existed prior to colonialism. It was the encounter of the God incarnated in Jesus Christ and witnessed to in the Scriptures that led to the development of Rukwadzano. In fact, it was precisely these women's encounter with the Bible that enabled their faith to transcend the negative images of their identities and their traditional culture taught by the missionaries.

In 1929, Lydia Chimonyo, a pastor's wife at Old Mutare, claimed she strongly believed in the power of prayer and in the Holy Spirit to change situations. She found eight other women who were pastors' wives and who shared her convictions. These women became the mothers of Rukwadzano in the Methodist Episcopal Church of the Rhodesia Mission Conference. The group started by gathering for prayer soon after fetching firewood out of the forest; then they agreed to set times and places for meeting twice daily for prayer.

They selected paDara in the east and paChingando in the south, both locations outside of the mission campus. Upon learning of this base community, or prayer group, and its leader, the leaders of the mission church grew very nervous and suspicious. As a result, the leaders of the mission church gave Chimonyo a hard time. They often asked, "Through whose wisdom and authority did this work begin?"

The uneasiness of the American missionaries was well founded, since African women intuitively sought to draw on their traditional roles, values, and experiences as African women. The Shona view of the world, out of which Manyika women came, gave them much authority in leadership roles. Their authority derived from their role in the family as *Tete* or *Semukadzi* (She-Head) in the family.

In what follows, I argue that the women who organized the original Rukwadzano had three critical themes central to their well-being and survival on their minds. First, they brought with them to the mission a desire to hold on to their traditional past, which they saw as sustaining them and their community in helpful ways. Second, they always sought to remember that mission education was forced on them by colonial powers. They resented being coerced to come to the mission school, because they witnessed the oppressive economic and political practices of the mission church. As a result, they quietly envisioned themselves as political refugees; and this identification later influenced what they gleaned about themselves from the Bible. Finally, they came to the mission not only to learn but also to search for a nurturing and redeeming community, given the disruption that the colonial occupation had on their lives. Rukwadzano was formed precisely because the mission church neither recognized nor acknowledged these three basic motivations and expectations.

During this period, women were aware that they were brought to the mission to be converted to a new religion as a conquered people. Disempowered and dispossessed, they soon identified with the "Babylonian experience" of Israel in the Hebrew Bible. When the mission church refused to listen to their yearnings for freedom, they began to visualize themselves in exile. Paradoxically, though it was the missionaries who introduced them to the Bible, it was the Bible stories about the bondage and exile of the Hebrews with which the women identified. They began to see themselves as people who "remembered Zion" and who wondered how they could "sing the LORD's song in a foreign land" (Ps. 137:1, 4).

The mission church quickly tried to silence these songs. Its strategy was to tame and domesticate this movement by superimposing the church's agenda, structure, and doctrine on the women. However, this effort did not stop the women. Drawing on what they brought from their Shona culture and the Bible, the women fashioned models of leadership and service that clearly defined their vision and mission in a new society and a new church. In their personal lives, at revival meetings, and at base-community meetings, the women witnessed, pledged, and committed to create a redeemed and healed community.

My mother, Ruwisa Nyakatawa Mutasa, recalls how, as a young woman, she joined the Rukwadzano meeting in which Lydia Chimonyo was preaching. She said:

> As young people, we would accompany our mothers to these revival meetings. Most of us went for fun as well as to help our mothers with child care or chores while they participated in these gatherings. One year, I had joined my mother to go to the Nyatande camp meeting, as I did every year. One afternoon I decided that, instead of staying at the *musasa* (shelter) with the other young people, I would join the women at the meeting already in progress.
>
> At first it was difficult for me to make sense of why Lydia Chimonyo and the other women preachers were jumping all over the crowd, preaching at the top of their voices to a silent crowd. I soon became aware that the audience was silent and spellbound because the whole place was charged with what can be called emotional energy. I do not remember what really happened on this day. All I remember is that at some point in the women's preaching I had started listening to their message and I liked what I was hearing. The meeting broke into song with traditional Manyika lyrics.
>
> Accompanied by a *hosho* (percussion instrument/rattle), the men were leading the song. During this time drums were allowed for use in

church music. From nowhere I broke into prayer, fell into a trance, and opened my eyes to find it was way into the evening. I could not tell how long I had been in that state nor could I tell what had actually happened to me. All I can tell you is that on this day I made a personal decision to take the Christian message as preached by these women seriously.

In 1958, while at Rusape, I became a member of the Rukwadzano in our local church at Mandisodza. Every Friday I made sure I was the first one to get to our weekly meeting with the other women. In this group we were not only personally healed but we also got the opportunity to go out and minister to others who were hurting like us.

I am deeply grateful that you found an opportunity to write on our movement/organization. The Rukwadzano is what I have breathed, eaten, danced, drunk, and slept all my life.[8]

It is clear from what my mother reported that these women experienced their religion and what was experienced was very personal. Yet it was in the context of a faith community where they were aware of their experiences in a colonial situation. Thus, what was taking place in their lives was divorced neither from the new faith nor from their traditional culture. What was taking transpiring was their encountering a new way to interpret what was occurring under oppression as well as helping them encounter God, whom they had already known. This new encounter with God became the means through which they took the essence of the Christian faith and translated it into their traditional culture.

Telling a New Story

The Unwritten Text is all about reconstructing and telling a story of how Shona women developed Rukwadzano, beginning with the European arrival and the founding of the Methodist Episcopal Church at Old Mutare. The story builds on interviews and primary-source material collected at Old Mutare Mission between 1992 and 1993. The late Mambo Abisha Mutasa and Mbuya Firipa Muchirahondo Nyajeka (then ninety-eight years of age) were critical to the process of reconstructing the involvement of Manyika women in their communities at the turn of the nineteenth century.[9]

The Mutupo view of the world of the Shona was reconstructed from a variety of sources including ethnographic history, oral sources—Shona folk-tales, myths, and legends—as well as a personal knowledge and experience of this culture.[10] Other sources include records at Old Mutare Mission of the Methodist Episcopal Church and at Church Archives at Garrett-Evangelical Theological Seminary, in Evanston, Illinois. Such sources of information will reveal the view of the world that Shona women brought to the mission church.

The chapters of this book build one on another as the story of the development of Rukwadzano is told. Chapter 1 reconstructs the Mutupo worldview that the Manyika women and men brought to the mission school. Chapters 2 and 3 focus on a typical portrait of Protestant missionary women, who were commissioned by the Woman's Missionary Society of the Methodist Church in the United States to begin work among Manyika women in Mutare, Zimbabwe. I will show that women from U.S. America came to Africa in the nineteenth century to expand their own voice and participation beyond Western prescribed roles, but they could not extend the same freedoms to those to whom they sought to bring Christianity. They were impeded in their efforts because they imposed a culture that ignored the indigenous culture that already existed.

Chapter 4 narrates how the missionaries adopted colonial myths about African women and tried to make African women into the image of Western white and European women. Chapters 5, 6, and 7 show how African women drew on their achievement of literacy and how their encounter with the God of the Bible and the incarnated Jesus Christ led them to the Rukwadzano movement. They were able to distinguish the essence of the Christian gospel from its Western cultural trappings and the colonial government tyranny. Finally, chapter 8 summarizes the movement's historical development and draws implications for present and future Zimbabwe and the West.

CHAPTER 1

The Shona Worldview: Shona Women before Colonization

IN 1890 THE BRITISH ENTERED THE TERRITORY OF PRESENT-DAY ZIMBABWE where the Shona and Ndebele lived. These groups shared a common religious view of the world that was centered around the Mwari cult at Matopos. According to this worldview, women were prominent participants and were viewed as equals in all matters of shaping the future and destiny of their people.[1] Through this religious view of the universe Shona women exercised power and authority that permeated all aspects of the life of their communities. Women were not just prominent priests at the shrine; they also held key political positions within the family, community, or clan.

During this period gender relations among the Shona, for the most part, seem to have been quite amicable and egalitarian. For example, in the nineteenth century it was a woman who acted as Mwari's oracle at Matopos. Political systems throughout the region consulted the oracle on all matters of state and culture. Emissaries were sent annually from the various regions to petition for rain and to seek counsel from the oracle on matters of polity and government. Moreover, young girls (*mbongas*) were trained along with boys (*hosanas*) to be the messengers of Mwari, and both would eventually marry into the various clans and assumed the role of *mhondoro* (Clan/*Mwari* Spirit) among the people. The power and authority of these female figures came into evidence and full expression in 1896–97 when Tekela wa Ponga and Nehanda Nyakasikana helped Mkwati and Kaguvi plan, organize, and execute the first *Chimurenga* (war of resistance) against British colonialism.[2]

Portuguese and British authorities also had to deal with women governors, who were prominent throughout the Shona territories. An example is Chikahga and her five sisters of the Mutasa dynasty in Manyikaland. Throughout the colonial period the British would deliberately undermine the power and authority of these women by annexing their land or ignoring them, despite the fact that their people continued to consult and recognize their political legitimacy.[3]

Power and authority were available not only to women from royal or priestly circles. Through the Mutupo principle, a majority of ordinary women were nurtured and trained to be comfortable with demanding and exerting power and authority at all levels of their cultural experience. In pre-colonial Zimbabwe, Shona and Ndebele women had more than access to land, power, and property. A rubric of formal and informal rules protected their rights as well as interests as mothers, wives, sisters, or daughters. Tonga policies in north-western Zimbabwe enabled women's powers of self-expression to flourish in all spheres of social influence.[4]

In most pre-colonial societies women enjoyed fundamental rights and privileges that were either abruptly lost or slowly eroded by colonialism and the colonial state.[5] One has to look in colonial and missionary sources to find interpretations of pre-colonial Shona policies as rigid patriarchies in which women were chattel and slaves who remained legal minors subordinate to men in all matters of existence.[6]

In this chapter, I analyze oral and written sources of Shona philosophy to show a Shona worldview in which women were nurtured to be comfortable with the pursuit of power, authority, and rights in their communities. In these polities, women were sages, hunters, politicians, counselors, artists, dancers, musicians, farmers, miners, business people, and mothers in their communities. I also address the following questions: (1) What kind of culture existed in Zimbabwe when the missionaries arrived? (2) Did the culture need a radical overhaul because of pagan practices incompatible with the Christian faith? (3) Are the ancient Mediterranean orientation undergirding the early church view of the world and the Shona orientation to the world compatible? (4) Was patriarchy, or a male-dominated world, the major orientation in Shona culture at the time the missionaries came?

The Mutupo Worldview around 1900 A.D.

Shona cosmology was two-dimensional in expression. First, Mwari shrines were constructed to symbolize the cooperative spirit of all of existence. Second, the Mutupo (totem) story of creation was elaborately constructed in order to affirm the uniqueness and individuality of entities, such as species, genders, clans, races, and categories, and to show the relationality of all this diversity within existence.

At the turn of the nineteenth century, Shona (and possibly the Ndebele) society was organized around the Mutupo principle, an overarching religious philosophy expressed in stories through which the Shona understood their lives in relationship to one another and the rest of the world.[7] The creation story embodies assumptions about life and about relationships between people and the divine and between people and nature and relationships with the entire world.[8]

Around the turn of the century both Shona and Ndebele societies organized their total reality around the Mutupo story of creation. From this story and the belief in a deity their societies derived understanding of science and an ethical and moral code that reflected their understanding of relationships in existence. In turn, this scientific understanding and ethical-moral code served to protect and perpetuate the people's worldview.

The Mutupo Story

The Shona creation story is at once simple and complex, providing a blueprint for understanding life and its meaning and providing Shona people with their sense of identity and their place in the cosmic scheme of things. It also served as the medium through which they experienced and expressed the meaning of existence.

There are three dimensions to the story, expressed in three beliefs. (1) *Mwari* (God) is the creator of nature and the universe. (2) The origin of some humans and creatures is aquatic. (3), The origin of other creatures and humans is terrestrial.

In his book *The Karanga Empire*, Chigwedere presents a simple outline of the Mutupo myth of creation for Shona people in present-day Zimbabwe. From this story he reconstructs a migration theory of the Bantu groups that settled in the area of present-day Zimbabwe. The Bantu groups that settled in the area, argues Chigwedere, held a common but distinctive story about their origin. The story centered around the Mutupo totem concept. The first group to arrive, around the eighth century, was the Karanga. They entered a land occupied by the Tonga; before the Tonga, it had belonged to the San people. Around the twelfth century, the Karanga were followed by a second distinctive group, the Mbire.[9]

The Karanga story of creation places the origin of life and existence in the Great Pool (*Dzivaguru*). In this myth the Great Pool (*Save*) is understood as the place of origin for all of nature and creation. Aquatic life points to the beginnings not only of the Karanga people but also of all life. To affirm this belief each clan is required to adopt an aquatic species and designate it as its originator or Mutupo (totem animal). For example, a clan may choose as its originator, or *Mutupo*, the hippo (*mvuu*), and another may choose the eel (*hunga*). Thus Karanga clans derived their distinctive identities from aquatic life. Other Mutupos include the fish (*Hove*); the water python (*Mheta*); the crocodile (*Garwe*); the Great Pool (*Dziva*), the fish-eagle (*Hungwe*), and the otter (*Mbiti*). According to Chigwedere, the uniting symbol for the Karanga clans is *Hungwe*, the fish-eagle.

The Mbire story of creation claims its beginnings on the land. Their story centers around the Great Monkey (*Soko*) concept. Here the clans derive their Mutupo from terrestrial species. Examples of Mbire clan Mutupos are antelope (*Shava*), termites (*Beta*), pig (*Humba*), elephant (*Nzou*), lion (*Shumba*), human female organ (*Tsivo*), and buffalo (*Nyati*). The monkey (*Soko*) is the uniting symbol of the Mbire group's understanding of the universe.

The Shona Worldview

Around the turn of the century the Shona viewed and experienced the world through the Mutupo principle. The foundational basis for this principle is the relationship of all of existence. Mutupo principle focuses on relationships and the nurturing of such relationships. It focuses on defining the primary relationships between animals and humans, animals and the deity, humans and humans, nature and humans, deity and humans, and the dead and the living. The Mutupo principle attempts to enumerate or approximate the ideal mode of existence, one that assures a sustainable future for all of existence. It seeks to describe the universe in ways that take the existence of humans and nonhuman entities seriously. In Mutupo story a clan adopts another species and covenants that "its people shall be our people." A solemn commitment to protect one another's survival is established with the human assumption that the nonhuman will understand. The identity and destiny of the clan and the Mutupo are perceived as congruous: whatever happens to one is viewed as directly affecting the other.

The relationship between the clan and its Mutupo is a sacred covenant. In this covenant the two parties understand themselves as agreeing to be faithful, loyal, and committed to affirming one another's life and existence. In the interest of guarding and protecting this symbolic relationship, a Shona worldview is constructed in which the Mutupo principle of relationships is regarded as the normative base for understanding human experience and knowledge. To the Shona, the mention of one's Mutupo evokes sacred meaning. It resonates with every dimension of human experience, including worship, security, justice, love, community, life, romance, praise, dance, death, motherhood, beauty, the living, the dead, and the yet-to-be-born.

The Fundamentals of the Mutupo Principle

There are three fundamental principles of the Mutupo story. Out of these three principles of the Mutupo story, a Shona moral code that attempts to grant and protect freedom for all of creation is constructed. First, there is a belief in the unity, or oneness, of all of nature and existence. Second, the Mutupo story communicates a view of the universe in which every entity is perceived as inherently endowed with freedom and some rights to be. Finally, God/Mwari is given as the source and sustainer of all of life and existence.

The Oneness of Nature

The Mutupo principle points to an intrinsic oneness/unity of nature. This oneness of nature is viewed as a status of egalitarianism of all of nature as existence. All of nature is perceived as imbued with an energy force that manifests itself in diversified forms as reality or nature. The Mutupo concept seeks to communicate this principle. It begins by establishing that humans, the deity, nature, time, and space are of the same essence. The nature of reality and existence defies hierarchical forms in every aspect and, instead, is an intricately bonded web of relationships. The circle accurately symbolizes this dynamic phenomenon, since it has no beginning and no end. Thus, space and time, fire and ice, humans and animals, women and men, young and old, deity and creation—all are related in a way that shows no beginnings or ends and no hierarchical structures.

This belief in mutual interrelation is communicated by commonly used idiomatic expressions like *"Mwana anozwara mai"* ("The baby gives birth to the mother") or *"Mambo wanhu"* ("Chieftaincy/leadership is the people").

The Shona worldview also communicates nature, reality, and existence as paradoxical mysteries of interrelationality rather than as a bipolar struggle of competing opposites. The challenge of existence is to seek to understand the nature of this interrelationality between, for example, earth and sky, women and men, young and old, fire and ice, deity and creation, and day and night. Emphasis on the relationality of nature and existence creates a worldview that is characterized as "ecological spirituality." Here dualism and the dichotomization of entities is negated. Instead, "Reality itself, while multifaceted and diverse, is better characterized as a vast network of interdependent and interfacing events than as a dualistic and dichotomized aggregate of mutually incompatible substances."[10]

A Right to be Free in Relationships

According to the Mutupo principle, everything in creation is free to be because it exists. Each entity in existence is inherently endowed with a right and freedom to be. This continuance of existence and the survival of species is entrusted to the custodial care of all of nature as creation. The Shona have prayed to the forest to be "kind and merciful" and return the children when they have wandered and disappeared in its thicket. Entities are viewed as of intrinsic value in and for themselves, even as they are of instrumental importance to others.[11]

Shona folklore and idioms encapsulate the history and nature of this dynamic way of relationality. In African folklore, every bush, rock, river, and animal has a character and a voice. Human beings never occupy center stage, nor are they considered the smartest characters in the story. Indeed, one may argue that Shona cosmology is "animal-centric," because in the folk tales humans are depicted as extensions, even caricatures, of animals or nature.

Take, for example, a story titled "The Hare and the Animals of the Forest," in *Mungoshi's Stories from a Shona Childhood*. The main characters in the tale are Lion, Elephant, Frog, and Hare. Typically, the setting for the story is a time of massive drought "in all the land." As a severe shortage of water sets in, Lion, the self-appointed "King" of the forest, calls a meeting of all the animals. Lion may be organizing the community for survival but the story leaves not doubt that Lion's real motivation is a lust for power. Thus, Lion's acts of community service have elements of self-aggrandizement because he/she (in the Shona language animals and humans assume a neuter pronoun) expects praise and glory from everybody.

Elephant's character is one who is wise and mature. Elephant carries her/his weight with grace and prudence. For example, Elephant recognizes Lion's self-appointed authority and agrees to be the first to tackle digging the dry ground. In the process of digging, he/she demonstrates patience and perseverance in spite of the dry dust still spewing out when the hole is so deep that all that the others can see is Elephant's back. All the large animals then take their turn after Elephant. The hole gets deeper but dust continues to spew mercilessly.

In spite of Lion's insults, anger at and denial of Frog's request for his/her turn to try (on account of Frog's size), it is Elephant, who, after a second thought, deems it just to give Frog a turn in digging the well. Later, it is Elephant who again prevails with the decision to commute Hare's death penalty for Hare's treacherous lies. Elephant, on the issue of the death penalty, prevents the community from having anyone's blood on its hands. Elephant is the collective conscience of a community laboring for the survival of all.

Frog's character symbolizes aspects of reality in which "animal-logic" is defied. Having been constructed by Lion as the self-appointed leader, "animal-logic" takes for granted that physical attributes of stature and size translate into power and authority to fulfill one's personal wishes and desires. Therefore, when Frog politely asks for her/his turn, not only does Lion reprimand and jeer at Frog but out of frustration and fatigue the other animals decide it is time for a lunch break. They were not even going to give Frog the honor of their supporting presence. While they are gone, Frog sings mournfully to the little hard rock at the bottom of the well, "Open up for me before my skin dries up." Suddenly the dust turns into mud and the mud into a gush of water coming out of a crack in the rock at the bottom of the well. The other animals come back to find Frog taking a *siesta*, supine at the top of a well of fresh water. The animals dance around the well, carrying Frog as high as they could. Lion is enraged for not getting the credit!

Hare's character symbolizes an individual who tests the moral fiber of a community. Hare is deviant, silly, lazy, and never serious about anything. Yet, Hare is also sweet, cunning, and friendly and considers him/herself related to every animal in the community. Hare refuses to participate in the well digging. All the plans employed by the community to deny him access to water prove a dismal failure. Once more, it finally takes insignificant Frog to ambush and capture Hare in the act of stealing water. The question for the community becomes whether Hare should be put on public welfare or put to death.

For Shona culture, such stories illustrate inclusive and democratic relations between different "types" of people in the community, where the small and clever may prevail over the self-acclaimed leaders.

Utopia

This world of animals in folk tales in Shona philosophy is a blueprint for Utopia. It is a genre of literature that initiates young children into the principles of democracy, freedom, peace, and justice. The law of this land has always been known as one of a consensual democracy in which meetings are called for and everyone's voice is expected to be heard before an agreement is reached. At an early age, the children are initiated into a consciousness of the ethical and moral dilemmas of life and existence. In the animal stories lie the existential dilemmas of choice between the community's and the individual's agenda. In these stories a child learns lessons on friendship, love, hate, the warmth of neighbors, courage, war, kith and kin, anger, greed, commerce, and frustration. It is also these stories that teach a Shona child to be merciful and kind.

Most Shona animal folk tales are set in a context of a severe drought, for two reasons. First, through these stories valuable scientific knowledge is transmitted to children, conditioning them to remember always that in Shonaland they dwell in a delicate ecosystem of periodic droughts that perpetually threaten all of life and existence. Second, a drought setting may form an analogy representing the nature of existence and the human condition in which survival is not a personal matter but one that requires the mind of a community. A child is taught *"Munhu Wanhu"* ("To be is community").

As illustrated above, Mutupo principle teaches the young not only to aspire for community but also to build democratic communities in which the rights and privileges of both the great and the small are recognized, where might is not always right, and where the powerful suffer the tyranny of the little ones. For example, when eating from a communal plate, Shona children are taught that the oldest gets the first bite and the youngest gets the last piece in the plate. Through animal characters, Shona children are taught the fundamental principles for survival in their environment. Again, as illustrated in the tale above, children are initiated into a consciousness of ethical and moral dilemmas in existence. Principles of democracy, freedom, and justice are thematic in these tales.

Shona idioms and folk tales tell the young that power and authority are measured by how far one is willing to make sacrifices for the peace and harmony of others and of the community and also for one's own desires and interests. The purpose and duty of the healthy and strong individuals in a community are to protect the weak and vulnerable in order to ensure everyone's well-being and survival. Thus, a child is taught that leadership is a role ordinarily shunned rather than aspired to, because one's assumption of leadership means a life wholly committed to the survival of a community in every way. It also means a life lived humbly through meditation, discipline, and self-denial, in which a loss of personal freedom becomes the norm. As a leader, one can no longer accrue personal wealth or property. Instead, the leader's wealth is commonwealth. For example, one of the nineteenth-century myths perpetrated by the British South Africa Company to justify the police raid of thousands of Ndebele cattle was that they were the "King's" and privately owned.[12] A leader may not justify any act of accruing and amassing wealth for private ownership. The Shona understand leadership to be a paradox in which the most revered by way of authority invested in them assumes the worst curse. The responsibility entailed in leadership is burden, a curse. A leader's life is expected to be lived for a community. There is a Shona saying, "*Ishe idurunhuru*" ("The chief is a rubbish pit").

Mutupo as Solemn Covenant

In the Shona understanding of the universe, one's Mutupo, or totem animal, becomes a symbol of a covenant relationship of all in the universe. Mutupo becomes a sacred covenant in which the human pledges to protect and enhance the life and survival of their "siblings" of another species. One's identifying with a totem animal is viewed as a self-emptying experience in which a species transcends an egocentric view of the universe and lives a life limitless in its existential experience. Shona poetry, art, dance, music, folklore, and philosophy express much on this experience from a human perspective. From childhood, children are showered with praise poetry and teased with gestures that imitate their totem animal so as to imprint this identity on them early on. Some early European settlers viewed with suspicion such praise and terms of endearment showered on babies and children as a method of child-rearing.[13] Such attention given to a child groomed an egocentric personality, they thought.

These praise names, poetry, and terms of endearment actually served to teach the child two fundamental aspects of the Shona view of the universe. First, through its Mutupo, the child belongs to a community larger than the human community. Second, the child can claim her/his place in the universe with pride because there were people before that child who had made the child's birth possible, and now it is the child's turn to live wisely. Such daily praise poetry does not end with childhood but is evident in the ordinary ways of Shona people. For example, Shona daily greetings serve as a constant reminder of the belief in the "trans-species" relationships of existence within the Mutupo principle. When a person whose totem animal is being greeted, whether male or female, and their totem is *svosve*/ant, they are addressed as *Mhukahuru* ("powerful animal"), *Chirombowe*, ("the powerful, awesome one"), or directly by their totem animal. For example, a greeting would go as follows:

"*Mangwanani Chirombowe Mhukahuru Soko!*"

"Good Morning, Awesome One/Monkey!"

This greeting conveys two aspects of Shona thought. First, taken literally, it is a praise poem to the existence of both a person (human being) and their totem (animal). The greeting celebrates the mystery of existence by mutually assuring one another that each has a place in the universe.

Second, this salute is an affirmation to the nature of this mystical relationship of nature. The idea poignantly communicated in this salute is one of the paradoxes of being human. Human beings would like to view themselves as the most awesome of all creation (*mhukahuru*), with the capacity to think freely and manipulate the environment.

However, they recognize that they share a common destiny with their totem animal as a fellow creature whose survival or extinction is dependent on the nature of community created in the universe.

The universe is viewed as having been created not for human exploitation but for sustaining all of creation. The Shona believe that when the baboon baby runs out of milk, the human baby will soon face the same predicament. Shona thought acknowledges that "*Kakara kununa kudya kamwe*" ("The health of one creature lies in feeding upon the other") is a way that mournfully accepts the vicissitudes of reality, such as death. Yet it does so in a way that triumphantly celebrates the mystery of the interdependent and inter-relational nature of existence. Everything in the universe belongs to a community in which, ultimately, all entities exist for one another, entwined in a web of relationships. The formidable challenge for humans becomes the search for this community that affirms the interrelationships of life and is committed to creating and sustaining a peaceable community. The notion of a peaceable community—thematic in Shona folklore, music, and folk tales—points to the belief that to ensure survival for all, justice and freedom should be the law of the land for every creature, woman, man, and child.

Out of this challenge and search for a peaceable community proceeds the whole system of taboos in Shona cosmology. Taboos (*zvinoda*) in Shona cosmology are rules and regulations designed mostly to create a peaceable community that protects the weak and the vulnerable and acts with justice. Among the Shona, the word *taboo* (*zvinoera/zvinoda*) translates as "sacred" or "unapproach-able." It does not have the connotations of "uncleanness," the "profane," or "prohibition." An act, object, or word is taboo insofar as it is perceived as temporarily or permanently in a liminal stage.[14] The weak and vulnerable, such as babies, rare plant and animal species, postpartum mothers, boys or girls at puberty, the sick or dead, are taboo; that is, they are "holy" or "unapproachable." Priests, chiefs, warriors, healers, and warriors are also taboo.

Certain words in the Shona language are taboo because words are viewed as things or ideas that can become reality.[15] For example, it is taboo to comment that a particular baby looks beautiful. All babies are regarded as inherently beautiful and not objects of personal aesthetic judgments. If one made such a comment in the presence of the elderly or the wise, a rhetorical question would be posed, "Do you want us to burn all the ugly babies (now that you have found the most beautiful baby)?" One is taught to refrain from making superlative comparisons of existence and reality, for to do so is perceived as a potential source of contention and strife in pursuit of whatever has been defined as the best, the ideal, perfection. Hierarchy in any shape or form is negated or rejected.

The Science of Totems and Taboos

Encompassed in this cosmology of totems and taboos is a science of a people. Contrary to claims in colonial literature, the cosmology of totems and taboos is not superstitious science. Rather, it is a world of a dynamic culture in which new discovery and ideas are openly solicited and then, after critical study, either embraced or rejected. A frequently used Shona saying, "*Chitswa chirimurutsoka*" ("Mobility/travel is the source of new ideas/knowledge"), points to the openness of the culture to new ways and ideas. The scientific worldview of Shona culture aims at creating sustainable communities for the future. These are to be achieved through justice, in which the historical experience of a people is gathered and in which the lessons of success and failure serve to instruct present and future behaviors. In his study of Zambia, Munday grasped this dynamic of the social-scientific nature of African cosmology:

> The African child has a very thorough education, although it does not take place within the four walls of a school. The child's social education has been touched on. He or she learns to behave in his/her limited social circle by example and by precept and receives a very thorough education in the endless lore of agriculture, bird, beast, and medicine. This part of a child's education is for the most part pre-scientific; it is true that he or she is taught medicines that are true evacuees, emetics, abortificients, and so on. All these are known and used. The bulk of the education about medicines is pre-scientific, however. For instance,

hare's dung is used as a medicine for diarrhea because of its firm consistency; and a prickly seed is worn on a string round the neck for dizziness because "that is what one's head feels like." There are medicines for obtaining the favor of one's superiors; medicines hung in granaries that are thought to kill a thief even though he may not touch any of them. There is even a medicine for preventing the trouble that might be expected at the birth of a child who "has two fathers."[16]

The tabooing of one's totem animal saved almost all species of fauna and flora from extinction in Shona society. In the Mutupo principle, as stated before, a human community covenants with a nonhuman species that "your people" (animal) shall be "my people" (human).

This covenant is very significant to both parties. On the animal side, to have the biggest predator (a human) on one's side gives a certain amount of assurance for survival, freedom, and a peaceful existence. On the human side, refraining from totem-eating is a mark of a spiritual discipline to resist the danger of a wanton lust that can lead to self-predation. The taboo against killing or consuming one's totem animal extends to the beliefs the Shona have against the killing or consumption of meat and other species or resources. The Mutupo principle measures the worth of a civilization by how well it is organized to enhance the well-being of elements within a community. At this point one can argue that according to the Mutupo principle, the law of the jungle is "survival of the weakest."

Sex Taboos

Human sexuality is one of the most celebrated aspects of Shona life in general. Sexuality is acknowledged as a source of pleasurable experiences that, at the same time, can bind a community together. From an early age, girls and boys were taught to appreciate their bodies at every stage of development and nurtured to feel comfortable with sensuality. Grandmothers as educators encouraged children as boys and girls to "talk sex" and to explore and feel comfortable with every part of their anatomy. Grandmothers are known to be the only people who can call every part of the body by its proper name. It is not uncommon to hear them shouting to a peer group of girls or boys sunbathing across the river, jokingly inquiring why their private parts look either too small or too big.

Sexuality is the subject of many Shona stories, tales, and legends, as well the topic of poetry, song, dance, jokes, gossip, and laughter. However, it is also in the area of human sexuality that one meets with a litany of taboos. The people's experience must have identified it as a source of disequilibrium in a community's search for a peaceable existence. Early missionaries, anthropologists, and psychologists focused much interest and speculation on these taboos on human sexuality. It is how most of them came to reduce, erroneously, the rationale behind these taboos as "the avoidance of incest." These European scholars also thought the Mutupo story had been reduced to the avoidance of incest and the promotion of exogamy, or marriage outside of specific groups.

Shona taboos on sexuality generally fit into two categories: avoidance taboos and abstinence taboos. Avoidance taboos are further divided into two categories. One category is designed literally to protect the weak from sexual molestation by the strong, while the other serves to create a temptation-free environment for the morally weak.

Avoidance Taboos

The taboo against any sexual intercourse with one's child, sibling, blood-relative, or even clan member (same Mutupo) can be justly termed the first commandment. Any sexual activity with one's kin is perceived as synonymous with the eating of one's Mutupo/totem animal.

The eating of one's Mutupo is considered cannibalism—an unbridled appetite or lust for the eating of one's own flesh. Such an urge is defined as the root of evil or *uroyi* (witchcraft). In cannibalism one is not only seeking to eat the weak ones of any kind but also devising methods for eating the whole community, including one's self. In Shona cosmology cannibalism symbolizes the beginning of the end for any community. As a result, cannibalism negates the Mutupo principle that aims at protecting the weak and the vulnerable. When cannibalism breaks out, only the "fittest" in the group may survive and those weak or viewed as weak will be devoured. Sexual intercourse with one's blood relatives or clan group is taboo because incest is perceived as a lustful appetite for power and control of the weak and vulnerable in a community.

In Shona law, there is no separation between civil and criminal offenses. For example, incest and rape are viewed as criminal violations of both the community and the individual. It is *zvinoera*, "sacrilegious." In some communities capital punishment has been meted out for these offenses. Rape or incest is viewed as a crime against community. The Shona believe that whenever such a crime has been committed by one of their own, the rains will not fall. Taboos on incest and rape are considered matters of a community in search of justice, peace, security, and freedom for its young and vulnerable. At the same time, it is a pledge by the "strong" elements to self-discipline, reverence for the rights of the other, and a commitment to the promotion of peace and harmony.

A second category of the avoidance sexual taboos are those designed to serve and protect the morally weak from temptation. These taboos attempt to safeguard against clandestine sexual liaisons, which have been known to be the origin of communal disharmony and tragedies. For example, it is taboo for a son-in-law to be in close physical proximity with his mother-in-law or to look into her eyes. The same goes for the relationship of a daughter-in-law to her father-in-law. The taboo also applies vice versa.

The young bride or groom who does not belong to the clan can be a potential source of sexual fantasies gone berserk either on their own part or on the part of the in-laws. Avoidance taboos guard against clandestine sexual relationships that threaten the whole community. Such taboos are gradually relaxed. After a long time in a marriage the son-in-law is said to have become a son and the daughter-in-law a daughter.

Abstinence Taboos

Abstinence taboos committed the individual to temporary or permanent abstention from certain acts or foods or the frequenting of certain places. For example, eating one's Mutupo was permanently tabooed. Specific rules and etiquette governed a married couple's sexual life. Apart from those rules that protected against marital rape, couples were instructed to pay strict attention to abstinence taboos.

Abstinence taboos appear to have been designed to protect individuals and the community from physical and psychological harm resulting from the consequences of unregulated sexual activity even within the sphere of marriage. Sexual abstinence taboos were public health regulations. For example, postpartum sexual abstinence was meant to protect the health of a woman after giving birth. During this phase she was medically referred to as *mutate*; that is, weak or vulnerable and susceptible to physical or psychological harm, and therefore taboo. Not only was the woman viewed as physically and psychologically unsuitable for intercourse, but sexual relations also raised the specter of another pregnancy. A postpartum woman was placed on a "medical" diet and her movement was restricted. For example, she was not allowed to go to public places or to mingle freely with the public for fear she would be exposed to disease or other forms of harm.

Directly and indirectly, these customs and regulations also served to protect the baby's health and welfare. Generally, therefore, postpartum sexual abstinence was a public health concern. It simply allowed a woman to recuperate physically from the trauma of the birthing process. Moreover, it ensured the long-term survival and welfare of both the mother and the baby by preventing an early pregnancy. It was primarily a birth-control method. Shona music, folklore, and idioms are replete with themes emphasizing dangers of unplanned pregnancies resulting from careless sex. Musicians and dancers play classical pieces like "*Gore mwana gore mwana*" ("Having a baby every year is unacceptable") as reminders to the community to practice safe sex.

Around 1900, Shona couples were expected to nurture a child until at least age five before considering having another child. Both the husband and wife were accountable in the event of an early unplanned pregnancy. Early postpartum sexual activity that led to pregnancies was known to be one of the causes of women's deaths and a high infant mortality due to malnourishment. A husband who engaged in such sexual activity then would easily be accused of "witchcraft." Postpartum taboos and beliefs served to keep couples from careless sexual activity that could result in a tragedy.[17]

Couples were also to refrain from sexual activity during a woman's menstrual cycle. The belief was that a woman was too weak and vulnerable to participate and enjoy intercourse during this period. A woman's menstrual blood whence life is spawned conjure up and are expressed within the Mutupo *Tsivo* (female-organ, representing the human animal). Menstrual and postpartum blood are depicted as lava flow that gives birth to new forms out of a kinetic energy so hot that it will incinerate or burn whatever it comes in contact with. Therefore, a man may not come in contact with such potency.

Gender in the Mutupo Principle

The Mutupo story presents a nonhierarchical view of the relationship between males and females. Karen Sachs has come close to an accurate analysis of the complex nature of nonhierarchical gender relationships in some African societies.[18] At the turn of the century, whether male or female, Shona children were born and socialized to claim their identity through one's Mutupo. Children were addressed by their Mutupo at birth, at marriage, and at death. As *Semukadzi* (she-heads), all girl children were socialized to assume leadership roles in every sector of the community. Shona history and narratives are replete with colorful characters of women who were warriors, politicians, hunters, founders of clans, and more. The most prominent examples at the national level during this period were characters like Nehanda Nyakasikana, a spirit medium who led the national uprising against the British in 1896, or Chikanga among the Manyika.[19]

The challenge for Shona society was the translation and transmission of the Mutupo concepts of gender egalitarianism at every level and situation. Methods in the form of taboos, customs on courtship and marriage, etiquette, and folk tales were elaborately detailed.[20] For example, folk tales were a method used to raise a child's consciousness on issues of gender equality. The intent of a popular genre of folk tales narrated to children nearing puberty was to reinforce the Mutupo concept that women and men are created equal. The motif and theme of these tales cast women as powerful, independent, self-reliant, and self-determining beings. The message seemed directed to young males who at pre-puberty and puberty develop physical strength and stamina that, if not properly channeled, could be translated into a weapon for control and self-aggrandizement.

A motif running through Shona folk tales that could provide a window to their understanding of gender relations is what one may call the "Princess Charming" motif. The motif permeates most tales on romance and courtship; and the setting, of course, is a beautiful village in the land of plenty. A daughter is thinking of getting married. She is the most beautiful (not necessarily physically) girl in the village or she is the King's/Queen's daughter. Neither she nor her aunts find a suitable young man in the village. The father prepares a feast and sends word around to all the young men to come and audition. All sorts of young men come and perform every trick under the sun to win the princess—but in vain. To every young man's surprise, Princess Charming picks out the least conspicuous character in the contest. One can say this is an inversion of the Western Cinderella fairy tale.

In this story the young man chosen usually has some attribute or virtue that can easily be overlooked—attributes such as kindness, humility/gentility, integrity, patience, wisdom, temperance, listening, playfulness, and jocularity. In the popular imagination, these virtues are considered antithetical to bravery, popularity, aggressiveness, fame, wealth, power, and intelligence. The story teaches young women and men virtues upon which a lasting peaceable community is founded, for the couple is viewed as the primary building block of a community.

Motherhood

Motherhood is depicted in the Mutupo principle as an act of ultimate sacrifice. It views motherhood as a woman's numerous sacrifices. First, she gives up her original residence in her home community.

Second, she is willing to endure the physical discomfort, pain, and suffering of pregnancy and childbirth. Third, the society acknowledges that women somehow end up with the perpetual task of physically and spiritually nurturing both the children and a husband. Finally, society recognizes that women reluctantly give genetic rights of their children to the husband's group.

Once acknowledged, a woman's suffering and sacrifice in motherhood becomes a delicate matter in the Mutupo principle. Such sacrifice and suffering are expected to be recognized daily and appreciated here on earth. Otherwise, Shona people believe, upon her death an unappreciated mother or abused woman's "vengeful spirit" will annihilate a whole people (husband's group). In other words, among the Shona motherhood is not only understood in terms of sweetness, patience, nurturing, joy, and forgiving but also in a way that acknowledges a woman's real experience of pain, frustration, anger, and drudgery involved in the mothering process. Shona boys and girls are reminded that they may pick a fight with their fathers at any time but never with their mothers, lest their mothers never forgive or forget words said in anger.

A religious sanction to curb "mother abuse" is the rite of *Kutiza Botso*. In this ritual, the child hopes to secure forgiveness from a mother he or she has violated in some manner. In this process the child is expected to exhibit public penance by dressing up in rags or sackcloth and covering him- or herself with ash. For a week the child is to wander through the whole village publicly confessing in detail the manner of transgression toward his or her mother. The child is expected to resort to public welfare for food and shelter. The community will assess the genuineness of the child's repentance and, if merited, will grant forgiveness. In turn, the community will petition the mother's forgiveness on behalf of the child.

Religion

Finally, the Mutupo myth is a religious philosophy because a Creator-Being (*Mwari*) is perceived as the author and ultimate enforcer of the principles of life and existence. The Mutupo principle mediates a deity who created and continues to create. Second, all of creation, including humans, is understood as agents of the ongoing process of creation. All of creation in relation to the Creator is also considered to be of equal status and worth.

Mutupo points to a deity who is deeply mysterious, never to be comprehended by the human mind. This mystery of deity is chanted in Shona music, poetry, prayer, and ritual. *Mwari* is commonly referred to as *Chibwe chitedza chinokwirwa newatanu* ("the large slippery rock that only the healthiest can climb"). At the same time, God is known to be the one who participates and intervenes in the affairs of the universe because God's being is manifest in all creation. Mwari is remembered as having miraculously fed *sadza* (the traditional dish) to the starving regional emissaries who had come to petition Mwari for rain at *Mutiusinazita* (the nameless tree) during the years of severe drought. Mwari is known as the protector and vindicator of all the afflicted, oppressed, and downtrodden. Mwari at times is referred to as *Pfuyanherera* ("the one who nurtures the orphaned").

Since all of nature is understood to be of divine creation, it is endowed with the mystery and energy of the Creator. This belief explains the Shona veneration of all creation. In this perspective rivers, pools, mountains, forests, and hills are subjects of poetry to be revered. In this worldview nothing is ordinary. Everything in nature—from the largest to the smallest—is viewed with awe and wonder. Images of the ant that killed an elephant are imprinted in a child's mind as a way of communicating the nature of egalitarianism in all of existence. The story of the ant who offered elephant shelter from the storm communicates the nature of symbiotic existence for survival of all of nature.

Shona philosophy also views nature and existence in terms of mutual and egalitarian relationships rather than in opposition or as hierarchical. For example, women are not perceived as the opposite of men; rather the two are viewed as intrinsically and mutually related. The same perception applies to God and creation; spirit and physicality; the living and the dead; young and old; space and time. It is at this point of the relationality of opposing entities that the Shona believe created things are capable of transcending their nature specificity to become the other. God is not only understood as an exclusive being but is said to become the Great Monkey for the Soko Mutupo people, or Lion for the Shumba people. Humans are also known as capable of transcending gender and physicality, even space and time. All of nature is regarded as of equal worth because all is understood as divine creation.

Those studying issues of gender, the environment, or most aspects of precolonial Shona understanding of the world need to be aware of the governing principle behind the Shona view of the world. The Mutupo principle was a blueprint upon which Shona relationships were based. As typical of any community or civilization, the egalitarian ideal of the Mutupo principle did not always totally translate into reality. Over time and in different contexts, certain customs could begin to undermine the objectives of the principle's original intent. For example, the custom of giving the "bride gift" (*roora*) to the girl's family upon marriage in some cases developed into a commercial transaction with the harsh colonial environment and the introduction of mercantile capitalism. Shona culture within the Mutupo principle was dynamic and, like most aspects of African studies, should be studied historically.

At the outset of the chapter I raised four questions that need to be addressed. The first question relates to the nature of the culture that existed at the time the missionaries came. The answer is that Shona culture was egalitarian, relational, holistic, and communal.

The second question is whether Shona culture needed a complete overhauling at the time the missionaries came. The answer is that a fuller understanding of Shona culture and practices gives a more complete picture of Shona culture than the missionaries grasped. The third question asked whether or not Shona culture was compatible with the biblical world that existed in ancient Mediterranean culture. Ancient Mediterranean culture was clearly communal in nature;

therefore, there existed a great deal of compatibility between their orientations to the world. Moreover, the concept of the deity in Shona culture was compatible with the image of God in the Hebrew Bible and in the New Testament.

Finally, patriarchal views did not dominate pre-colonial orientations toward gender as was often assumed. Rather, equalitarianism and mutuality in gender relationships were the norm.

CHAPTER 2

The American Protestant Missionary

THIS CHAPTER RECONSTRUCTS A PORTRAIT OF THE TYPICAL EARLY PROTESTANT missionary woman who, like Mrs. Helen Rasmussen of the Methodist Episcopal Church, came to southern Africa from the United States at the turn of the century. It is a study of the late-nineteenth-century U.S.-American missionary woman's self-understanding, world-view, and theology—sources from which she drew instruction for work and ministry among the "native" women. Rosemary Keller and Patricia Hill have shown that these women were a product of the birth, growth, and development of the Protestant Women's Missionary Societies of the nineteenth century.[1]

The post-Civil-War period saw the greatest organization of women for causes in U.S. history. During this period the Women's Missionary Societies likewise emerged stronger and more focused on their mission in the Protestant churches in the United States. In the area of foreign missions, the women founded new societies, demanding not just a place for single women in the field but also autonomy on matters of their organization. In this exercise, the women expanded their sphere of activity and influence from the home to the public world and even overseas. The American Protestant women's theology of mission to women in the "heathen lands" during this period is imbued with a triumphalist spirit.[2]

A Historic Meeting

In June 1899, Mrs. Helen E. Rasmussen was commissioned and assigned to Old Mutare, Rhodesia, by the New York Branch of the Methodist Episcopal Woman's Foreign Missionary Society. Soon after her arrival, Rasmussen planned a trip for a long visit with Chikanga, the territorial governess of the area where the church had built its mission center. Her commissioning was a response to an urgent call from Bishop J.C. Hartzell, upon his founding of the East Central Mission Conference, for a woman missionary to begin work among the Manyika women.[3] Mrs. Rasmussen came to Old Mutare by way of the Madeira Islands, where her deceased husband had been a missionary. The Society was grateful and enthusiastic to have her commissioned because not only did Mrs. Helen Rasmussen have the advantage of experience in mission work on the African continent but also, being a widow, she calmed the anxieties of those in the church who were still uncomfortable with the sending of single women as missionaries into the foreign mission field.

Helen Rasmussen was a product of the long struggle of the nineteenth-century U.S.-American Protestant women's quest for a voice and full participation in the church. Becoming missionaries to foreign lands can be termed the pinnacle of their quest for involvement. The requirement for commissioning of this first group of women as foreign missionaries was that they be married. As partners to their husbands, these women would define, shape, and implement a Christian ministry among the women and children of foreign cultures. For example, Helen Rasmussen would be the first woman missionary to carry this out among the Manyika at Old Mutare at the turn of the nineteenth century. The first women to graduate from her school would later organize the Rukwadzano movement in 1929.

Upon arrival at Old Mutare in 1899, Mrs. Rasmussen reported back home that, as a prelude to her work, she had planned a long visit to Chikanga.[4] The purpose of her visit, she said, was to learn the Manyika culture and language. Rasmussen gives little information about Chikanga. In fact, Chikanga was one of the five Manyika women territorial governors of the Mutasa dynasty in whose territory the mission had been established. As mentioned in chapter 1, women governors were very common in many Shona polities in the nineteenth century.

By 1899, Chikanga had settled for a quiet political detente with the British. Nehanda Nyakasikana, the woman co-leader of the Shona *Chimurenga* (resistance), had been executed in Harare by the British three years earlier. According to H. Bhila, the "Chikanga Affair," which took place during this decade, had been read by the Mutasa people as signaling the end of an era.[5] In January 1894, Chikanga's husband, Fambesa, the military general and counsel, was shot and fatally wounded at the door of the royal residence by G. Seymour Fort, British-South Africa Company magistrate at Mutare. Fambesa died almost immediately. Accompanied by a police force, Fort had come to demand Chikanga's compliance with his ultimatum that she produce labor for the mines within forty-eight hours. Her resistance not only cost her a husband and a military general but also registered very clearly to her and her people that the British had finally conquered the region. Chikanga's political genius, fame, and prestige were legendary among her people. For over a decade Chikanga, her sisters, and their father, Chief Mutasa, had employed every political strategy in an attempt to keep both the Portuguese and the British from their territory.

Accompanied by three carriers, Rasmussen arrived at Chikanga's residence after a seven-mile walk from the mission. She was met by a male missionary who had gone ahead of her to build a hut in which she planned to stay for two months. According to the account, Chikanga greeted her "most graciously" and welcomed her to her "kraal" with great hospitality. This was a cause of great relief. However, she proceeded to describe the general unpleasantness of the condition she had entered. She set the stage for the beginning of her missionary adventures in Manyikaland as follows:

> Mr. Springer [whom she later married], who built the hut, went away and it was for the first time in my life I was left alone in a heathen kraal. I confess now, what I would not have admitted then for worlds, that I did feel afraid. And had I known of the dance that was on that night, I should have been still more afraid. Ignorance in that case was bliss. But He that watched over Israel neither slumbered nor slept; and so no harm came to me.[6]

Rasmussen's stay with Chikanga was fruitful. At the end of her visit Chikanga gave her a young girl, her niece Shakeni, to take with her to the mission. This was with the consultation and consent of both Shakeni and her mother. Shakeni would be the first Manyika girl at the Old Mutare mission. The two "friends" agreed that Shakeni was going to help Rasmussen around the house; and Rasmussen, in turn, was free to teach Shakeni whatever she pleased.

Chikanga and the mother's "giving away" of Shakeni to Rasmussen is a clear indication that all was not paradise in Manyika society. There were individuals within the socio-religious system with neither security nor place. Due to a certain inalterable human condition they were vulnerable to ostracism, discrimination, and oppression. Apparently, individuals like Shakeni had limited powers for self-determination or the freedom to make personal choices. An arbitrary decision, as in this case, could be made for them by those in authority. The presence of such elements of systemic marginalization of particular individuals within a community or culture usually portends its demise. In this case, ridding the Manyika community of some "ill-fitting" individuals, while not quite the end of the society, surely signaled the beginning of its demise.

Chikanga likely did not grasp this paradox. The claim that all of the girls who turned up at the mission were runaways fleeing from sexist, dehumanizing indigenous customs became an overriding theme within the Southern-African missionary sources. This myth, namely, that all Manyika women were marginalized and oppressed, became the basis upon which Rasmussen and the southern African church constructed their ministry for women. In this case early missionary women, in their zeal for converting and "civilizing" the southern African woman, collaborated with the male missionaries and colonial society in concealing the power, influence, and authority African women had in these societies. Instead of identifying, tapping into, and taking advantage of the sources of women's power in Shona or Ndebele societies, the church chose to join the colonial culture, which demeaned the power African women had in their societies.

Thus, in the early colonial literature African women are labeled and portrayed as witches. For example, Nehanda Nyakasikana was tried and executed as such by the British in 1897. In *King Solomon's Mines*, Henry Rider Haggard (1885) creates the character Gagool, who depicts the African woman as a demonic witch to be conquered en route to the source of gold. In later literature, Zimbabwean women would be depicted as drunks and prostitutes.[7]

The Making of an American Missionary Woman: 1900–1940

Old Mutare: Zimbabwe—16 November 1901

Of the eighteen people who appeared on the official picture of the first East Central Conference of the Methodist Episcopal Church meeting at Old Mutare in November 1901, six were women, two were babies, and eight were men, including the bishop. The two "native" evangelists, George Mpondo and Tizore Navess from the Inhambane District, are in the picture but their names are left out. Four of the women were married, the fifth widowed, and one was single. The widow was Helen Rasmussen, the recently commissioned woman missionary of the Methodist Episcopal Church's Women's Missionary Society. On the roll of persons in attendance recorded in the conference minutes, the married women's names, except for the prefix "Mrs.," were entirely their husbands' names. Bold asterisks appeared after the name of each woman and "native" evangelist denoting that officially they were "not members of the conference." The "native" woman was in neither the picture nor the minutes.[8] This picture and these minutes capture the birth of the social dilemmas the Christian church would have to struggle with in southern Africa in the years ahead.

On the subject of early women missionaries, the minutes obfuscate a number of crucial historical facts by labeling these women as nonmembers of the conference. Overall, such a characterization serves either to diminish or deny the role of Protestant and Catholic women in introducing and founding Christianity among the Africans in the nineteenth century.[9] First, by portraying women acting in the shadow of their husbands, the East Africa Conference of the Methodist Episcopal Church was in line with the "mainline" Protestant Church tradition of the nineteenth century, which discreetly concealed the fact that a majority of the women who married male missionaries were equally answering a call to a ministry in the foreign field.

Second, these minutes also obscure the fact that during this period the married women who entered the foreign mission field were trained as teachers, nurses, or doctors and understood their professional training to be tools for effective Christian ministry, a ministry to which they had been called. Finally, again, the portrayal of missionary wives as shadow, or "non-official," missionaries to the conference served to trivialize the women's ministry and thus deny them of any claim for future credit in the founding of Christian communities in the foreign mission field. The Protestant church was also refusing to acknowledge that, in almost all the foreign contexts, a women's ministry had become indispensable to the creation of what the church understood as authentic Christian communities. Only through the agency of women missionaries could this objective be accomplished.

Ideal Portrait

The conference minutes allow one to construct an "ideal portrait" of an early woman missionary for the Methodist Episcopal Church at the turn of the century. In the context of a church at a formative stage in Zimbabwe, she was to come to the foreign field first as a wife, second as a mother, and finally as a partner in ministry to her husband. Helen Rasmussen fit this portrait while serving with her husband in the Madeira Islands before coming to Mutare.

The early Protestant Church of southern Africa considered Mary Smith Moffatt, wife of Robert Moffatt of the London Missionary Society and missionary among the Tswana at Kuruman, South Africa, the ideal portrait of a woman missionary/wife. Her life and works became the model other early missionary women were expected to follow. In turn, these great women would use the "Mary Moffatt model" to fashion the "native" women into "ideal" wives, mothers, and workers. The Methodist Episcopal Church's Biblical Institute/ Seminary at Old Mutare, which trained all the pastors for the church, offered a required course on the life and work of Mary Moffatt. This course was meant to instruct and inform the new pastors on the work and role of women in the new religion.

This early model of a Protestant woman missionary as wife developed in the United States and Europe in the nineteenth century. Studies by Pierce Beaver and Leonard Sweet into the birth and development of this model in the history of Protestantism in the United States show that the model was replete with strengths, conflicts, and weaknesses. It was passed on as an ideal for the wives of the American missionaries at Old Mutare and then to the African evangelists and ministers and their wives as new converts to Christianity. In what follows, I show that in the context of an escalating colonial and racially segregated society, the benefits of promoting such a social ideal as liberating for African women became an elusive dream for the church, not only at Old Mutare but also for southern Africa as a whole.

A Woman's Call to Mission

The American Board of Missions (followed by others) became the first to reach the decision that "missionaries should, as a general rule, live in a married state, wherever they can obtain settled and undisturbed residence." Reasons for the general "rule of marriage" were spelled out as well as the qualities necessary for a suitable candidate for a missionary wife. These reasons related to how missionaries should live among their colonial subjects. Notes Beaver,

> The Christian familial and social duties cannot be exemplified before the heathen "unless missionaries, who are married to well educated and pious females, who have formed all the habits and modes of thinking in a Christian country," demonstrate those concretely in family life and general deportment. Moreover, missionary societies who strive to raise up a Christian population in the heathen lands where children are like "wild asses" or "colts," ungoverned, ungovernable, idle, and dissolute. Missionaries, in contrast to pagan parents govern and educate their children, make them learned, and can fit them also to be missionaries in their turn.[10]

A number of missionary children would indeed become champions or key participants as the American Board also felt that the marriage of missionaries would introduce to the heathens "the decencies of civilized life," such as "the appreciation of the female character."[11] By this they simply meant that the missionary household would become a model for the newly converted communities to emulate. On the matter of teaching the heathen "the appreciation of the female character," one cannot help but wonder whether the board was preaching this message to itself. Even the use of a phrase such as "the appreciation of the female character," reveals a Board that may be deliberately distorting the quest of the women of its own culture. Western women who ventured into the foreign mission field were looking for something deeper and larger than "the appreciation of the female character."[12]

The major condition for women's acceptance into the foreign field as missionaries during this period was that they be married. The missionary boards made this requirement very clear in its "marriage clause." The clause set out a clear profile of the character, training, duties, and obligations of the missionary wife. Desired qualities included "education," "personal conversion," and "piety." Her duties and obligations included being a minister to women in foreign lands, wife to her missionary husband, and mother to her children.

The marriage clause provided the Protestant church with a perfect strategy for doing missionary work and for accomplishing its objectives without compromising its ecclesiastical structure and its belief in the exclusive rights of men to leadership. In the foreign mission field the church would harness and benefit from the power of women's resources, both at home as money raisers and abroad as missionary wives, while continuing to view women as marginal to its ministry. The marriage clause allowed the church to permit women as partners in ministry discreetly without officially recognizing their ministry. Some early women missionaries in the field acted as if they were oblivious to this tradition and were quite comfortable in claiming the power and authority. For example, even though Helen Rasmussen (Springer) is listed as a nonmember of the conference of the Central African Methodist Episcopal Church, she insisted that Manyika women address her as *Mufundisi* (Pastor or Teacher), the same title carried by her husband.[13]

Another example of this ambiguity is Mrs. E. H. Richards, stationed at Inhambane. She understood herself to be both a minister of the gospel and a wife to her husband. In her report she shows that it was the work, beliefs, and lifestyle of these missionary women, and not the official church, that would judge their place in history. Their work left indelible marks on the communities they helped found in southern Africa.

By requiring an educated woman for a missionary wife, the nineteenth-century Protestant church is to be applauded for at least implicitly recognizing that women were graduating from professional academies and seminaries and therefore needed positions of employment. Until the birth of the various women's missionary societies, the heroic sacrifices of women as co-pioneers in the foreign field remained largely unheralded by the church.

With this courtship and marriage background, the missionaries in the foreign field would strongly advocate for courtship and marital relationships that repressed all open expression of affection toward a partner. Young men and women who joined the mission community would be encouraged to "pick" each other, marry, be assigned to an outstation, and live happily ever after. The new converts would pattern their marital relationship after their "teachers." The women viewed themselves as partners in ministry, but as wives, subordinate to their husbands.[14]

Conversion and Sacrifice

Courtship and marriage were accompanied by an emphasis on conversion and sacrifice. The missionary woman's conversion experience consistently reflects the evangelical tradition. The reports of most of the women at the East Central African Conference of the Methodist Episcopal Church (1901–10) begin with an account of her conversion experience, followed by the struggle as she is called to "surrender all" to the foreign mission field. For example, the only medical doctor in the whole group, "Mrs." (as she is addressed) F. D. Wolf, testifies that "mission and heathen are the two words she remembers hearing in her youngest days."[15] The result, she said, "was an impressed feeling of a special relation for the heathen."

First, her struggle was to choose whether or not she can "convert" because her understanding was that a conversion was followed by a sacrifice. She says,

> I am sure I would have been converted long before I was, for often when under conviction and about willing to surrender myself, the thought would come to me perhaps you will have to do something you are not willing to do, the foremost fear being the Foreign Mission Field.[16]

After her conversion at age thirteen, Wolf's strategy to avoid the call to any form of sacrifice was to steer clear of a missionary gathering "if I had even the merest excuse for remaining away and even if I did attend I would not take part in the service, not even to help sing."[17] Instead she diverted her energy to Sunday-school work, paying her mission money regularly, and persuading herself there were plenty of heathens in Cleveland among whom she could work.

A stay at her home by the Woodsides, missionaries to Africa, during Wolf's high-school years resulted in a voice that would not be quieted. In his prayer just before leaving to return to Africa, Mr. Woodside prayed that God would make someone in the Wolf family a missionary. Wolf answered this call four years after finishing medical school. Thus, in 1899, she and her husband left for Mutare, Zimbabwe.

Likewise, Mrs. Dewitt testified how, "in the winter of 1899, while attending a meeting in Huron County, Ohio, she sought and found Christ as a personal savior.'" Her joining and participation in the Student Volunteer Band as a student at Ohio Wesleyan University led her to believe that her "life work was in the foreign field, and that there, the Lord wanted me to be."[18] However, unlike Mrs. (Dr.) Wolf, Dewitt viewed her call into the foreign field not as a sacrifice but as a response to God's call to mission.

In their reports the women were explicit that their conversion experiences were to be understood as a mandate to their calling into the church's ministry. This evangelical experience served as glue that held a structure of many parts together. These women missionaries did not seem to have had problems with declaring their ministry as equal to that of their husbands; yet, at the same time, they silently accepted a subordinate position in church polity and politics. Wolf's emphasis on her conversion experience rather than on her professional achievements may have served to ameliorate what Barbara Welter describes as the threat to male missionaries posed by an influx of women doctors into the foreign mission field near the end of the nineteenth century.[19]

Equal but Subordinate

Missionary wives under this nineteenth-century partnership model understood themselves as equal partners in the ministry in relation to their husbands but did not overtly articulate any desire for equality in status in the religious or social arena. The women's opportunity to enter the foreign mission field to work with "their sisters in heathendom" came to be understood, by both men and women, as a natural situation whose solution lay in the division of labor along gender lines. In this arrangement missionary women in the foreign field would assume duties and responsibilities similar to those their husbands held, but they continued to be perceived and treated as subordinate by both the church and their husbands. As wives, missionary women would pass on this legacy—women seeking equal participation but not equality of status in matters of religion and society—to women in indigenous cultures.

Patricia Hill argues that nineteenth-century Protestant women were not seeking equality with men but were simply desiring to expand the household sphere to which they had by tradition been confined. She argues that a view of these women as radical, or "feminist" in the sense of demanding equal rights or entry into the public sphere, is not only false but also misleading. During this period, says Hill, women (like Catherine Beecher) as educators and philosophers clearly articulated the self-definition and self-understanding of "mainline" Protestant womanhood.

The Condition of the African Woman

Women missionaries held two views of the condition of the nineteenth-century African woman. The first and most popular is what might be called the "missionary-colonial myth." This view has prevailed in most southern African written sources. When writing to their home audience, missionary women to southern Africa and other parts of Africa, like their male counterparts, generally depicted the African women as the most depraved of humanity. African women were cast as "beasts of burden" who were bought and sold at childhood into polygamous marriages. In his *Africa Diamond Jubilee Documents*, penned in 1909, Bishop Hartzell put this view succinctly: "Like all pagan countries, womanhood is degraded. Wives are purchased and polygamy is common. A man's wives are reckoned with his other possessions. Practically the man's wives are slaves of their husbands, the wives perform all drudgery."

In the context of colonial southern Africa, this view served to justify the church's need for mission work among the women to "emancipate" them. It also developed into a myth with which the colonial government elites formulated policy and created laws fitting their view of the situation of African women. Proponents of the view also generally believed that Africans had no real religion, only a primitive pantheistic system of superstitious beliefs in magic and witchcraft. Bolstered by this belief, most missionaries also justified any means necessary to pull Africans out of this condition of perceived misery and superstition. Colonialism was viewed as a justified means to prepare the continent for evangelization.

The second view is precise and clear but unpopular. According to this view, African women are free, independent agents whose influence is felt at every level of their communities' cultural experience. Although proponents of this view were in the minority, they were for the most part not afraid to swim against the current of the harsh colonial environment. These individuals tended to acknowledge that Africans had a religion whose fundamental beliefs were somewhat similar to those of the Hebrews. However, most proponents of this view justified conversion by arguing that Christianity was a more enlightened faith suitable for the "new European civilization" that, generally, they considered somewhat superior to the indigenous religion. Some voices in this group strongly supported the "Europeanization" of the new converts.

The latter group contended that the task of evangelization and conversion was going be a challenge in any context, colonial or non-colonial, because the Africans appeared indifferent toward such efforts. A few of these missionaries began to disapprove strongly of African colonization. This process, they said, was not necessary for the evangelization of the continent. There was also a general consensus that the task of evangelizing the women depended on women missionaries. For example, in her article in the *Heathen Woman's Friend* in July 1879, Miss M. A. Sharp, missionary in Liberia, urges the Women's Missionary Society at home to "send your strongest women here. Mexico and Africa, although totally dissimilar, need the strongest characters, in order to make an impression that will be felt."[20]

The second view on the condition of the African woman was closer to the reality of the Manyika or southern African woman around 1900. In Manyikaland, women missionaries as wives would encounter an indigenous culture that contradicted every principle of the Puritan/Victorian ideal of womanhood they believed to be Christian. In the majority of non-Muslim Africa, missionary women would not find *Zenanas* or *Purdah*. The separate-sphere ideology was not part of these cultures. Men and women worked side-by-side in the fields and as brothers and sisters raised each other's children, mixed freely as social equals, and, in the warm evenings, danced and drank together. Mrs. Rasmussen describes the situation at Chikanga's as follows: "All the people, even the babies, drink beer. Soap is all but unknown, and the children wear most abbreviated clothing. The nights are spent in drinking, dancing and hideous songs. The great soul needs of the people [are] apparent."[21]

To most of the early missionary women, the condition of the African woman appeared largely ambiguous. This conclusion is supported by a general consensus these early missionaries expressed about the task of converting African women to Christianity. With their Victorian ideas on gender, early missionary women could not reconcile with a context in which a woman's place was not clearly defined.

Yet women such as Chikanga of the Mutasa chieftaincy proved that women held positions of power and authority at every level of Shona society. The *Manyika Washe* (she-governor) affirmed womanhood in a radically revolutionary way. Bhila explains how this practice (common among the Shona) permeated the Manyika political system:

> After consulting the *Semukadzi* (she-head), the clan spirit medium, the king appointed one of his daughters or sisters to one of the wards, or as a replacement of the dead ruler. Unlike the spirit medium, the women are allowed to marry and live with their husbands, who, as a consequence of their wives' position, acquired the title of *"nehanda"* (prince). These women were notorious for their permissive morals but their capacity to govern was strong. They were accorded great esteem.[22]

By 1875, there were as many as nine of these female governors in the Mutasa reigning dynasty: Kanganya, Rukuru, Manunure, Wisa, Mpotedzi, Risineuta, Nyakuwanikwa, Chikanga, and Muredzwa. Manyika women were politicians, judges, priests, traders, mothers, artists, and owners of property.[23] Women had equal claims to the communal ownership of land and cattle. In both patrilineal and matrilineal societies marriage customs were religious laws designed to prohibit strictly female abuse and to promote a woman's rights at every stage of her life. All these elements may have been quite elusive to the early missionary women who, for the most part, lacked reliable written sources on African culture or proficiency in the local languages. Women missionaries were largely on their own as far as ascertaining the situation of women in these communities.

Some of these missionary women could not help but highlight for the audience back home elements of an experience of culture shock in encountering southern African gender relations. Take, for example, an article appearing in the "Family News" section of the 1897 issue of the *Heathen Woman's Friend*:

> A Zulu woman's hut is her castle, and she will shut the door even on her husband. Miss Colenso says, "I have heard an angry woman say to her spouse; 'Not a scrap of food shall you eat to-day!' and he slinks away meekly." By a kind of a leap year arrangement a Zulu girl may without embarrassment propose marriage to any young man upon whom she set her heart.[24]

After taking over teaching some of the classes that her husband had started at Kambini in the East Central Africa Conference, Mrs. E. H. Richards was not comfortable with what she called the "closeness of the sexes." She proposed a solution to "this problem": "I am more and more convinced that the African boys and girls should be entirely separated in their schools."[25] The solution would be to create strictly separate spheres for boys and girls on the same campus throughout all their educational experience. A majority of the early missionaries could not easily adjust to and were paranoid about the nonsexual intimacy and free mingling of sexes within African communities.

Mrs. Helen Rasmussen

In her book *Snapshots from Sunny Africa*, Rasmussen, writing under her remarried name, Helen Springer, chronicles some of her early impressions of the Manyika women and Shona culture. Interestingly, Bishop Hartzell wrote the introduction to the book. According to Rasmussen, the bishop had insisted she "collect and work over into book form the many stories and articles" that she had been writing for various publications back home. Bishop Hartzell begins the introduction by quoting British general Baden-Powell, who, in a foreword to a book by Caroline Kirkland, wrote,

> How I should like to be a woman! It must be nice to lie back in your cushions and watch the men doing things which they think very clever, knowing all the time you can do much better yourself if you care to try.... Hence it comes that when women travel into the lesser-known countries of the world, as they frequently do nowadays, they bring this power of observation into play with remarkable results. And of all women in the world I would place our American cousins at the top of the list for this particular quality.... Unfortunately it is only too seldom that they record their impressions but when they do, their pages ripple with little touches both quaint and human which are the direct result of quick observation and which go to paint the character of the countries and the people far more vividly than the more erudite writings of a mere man who plods along basing his remarks very largely on what he has already read or been told of the country now spread before him.[26]

The themes in Rasmussen's *Snapshots from Sunny Africa*, as well as her reports to the Women's Foreign Missionary Society, show that she adopted the first view on the condition of the African woman. She chose the popular colonial/missionary myth to portray the condition of the Manyika/Zimbabwean women and their culture. In this book Rasmussen, in a clever way, selectively highlights aspects of Manyika life that portrayed the condition of Manyika women as inhuman and their culture as degenerate. She succeeded in this process of myth-making by either ignoring or neglecting any aspects that contradicted the image she was portraying. In her writings Manyika women are physically unattractive, mentally primitive/ savage, and filthy and wild but ultimately capable of being tamed to docility through coerced marriages. These first women missionaries saw their mission as one of freeing women from the drudgery of manual labor and "slave marriages" and moving them toward respectable "womanhood."

Rasmussen's attitude and interpretation of Manyika women and culture resembled those of her predecessors. For example, in her writings, Mary Moffatt constantly commented on how she was repulsed by most of the Tswana habits.[27] Like colonial women and male missionaries, early women missionaries deemed Shona culture grotesque and unsophisticated. For them, Shona culture was incompatible with what they called "Christian Civilization," which was being introduced by both the church and European colonization. It is at this point-the attitude toward the indigenous culture and worldview—that the church and the colonists in southern Africa formed a symbiotic relationship, or what in Zimbabwe one might characterize as a fervent romance. At this stage in the region the words *European, Christian, civilization*, and *white* were viewed as almost interchangeable.

The church used its relationship with the colonial powers to retain or expand its mission in most of the territories. The colonists, on the other hand, sought the church's endorsement of their notion of "colonization for civilizing." This situation was well articulated in President Roosevelt's address, given at the Africa Diamond Jubilee at the Metropolitan Methodist Episcopal Church in Washington, D.C.,

January 16, 1909. After personally congratulating Bishop Hartzell for the commitment to mission work in Africa, Roosevelt set out to define the task of church mission in colonial Africa:

> The white man rules; but there is only one white man to one hundred others, who are either barbaric black heathen or fanatical Mohammedans. . . . Civilization can only be permanent and continue a blessing to any people if, in addition to promoting their well-being, it also stands for an orderly individual liberty, for the growth of intelligence, and for equal justice in administration of law. Christianity alone meets these fundamental requirements.[28]

A tragic error occurred at this initial stage when women missionaries overwhelmingly chose to adopt the dominant view that labeled all African culture evil and completely irredeemable, with its women as the most victimized. This resulted in the church's failure to recognize and identify elements that were unique and useful for the founding of a relevant and effective ministry in Africa. Such a positive study among the Manyika could have ascertained and accurately established the role of women in this society.

Race and Culture

The adoption of this negative view by early women missionaries in southern Africa helped to fan the flames of colonialist, racist attitudes and policies in the region. In their writings, early missionary women in this region emphasized the "otherness" of African women in terms of color and culture and would never claim a solidarity of sisterhood along the lines of gender. The early articles featured in the foreign missions magazine of the Women's Missionary Societies conjured up images of a savage, wild, and primitive land. Women were mere "chattel" and "beasts of burden."

The early articles from Africa submitted to the *Heathen Woman's Friend* appeared under the heading "From the Dark Continent." In these early missionary writings the term *dark* was often charged with racial overtones. For example, in her book, Mrs. Rasmussen plays with this notion of color when describing the two donkeys they owned and took on the trail to Sena. First, there is the old donkey named Jack, who is described as a "gentle, sociable, reasonable, friendly little beast, an ideal lady's riding donkey." Then there is the newly purchased donkey who "was as black as Jack was white, so he was called Nig.' Nig is described as 'unbroken ... always kicking and squalling' of which he got in trouble."[29] To capture the "savage" image of the "Dark Continent," the first article in the "Family News" section starts, "There are supposed to be 20,000,000 cannibals still in Africa."[30]

Women and the Politics of Cattle

A majority of early women missionaries depicted the condition of African women as mere chattel, "beasts of burden," and victims of polygamous or coerced marriages. Generally, such opinions were borrowed from male explorers, settlers, and missionaries of the period. Settlers, explorers, and missionaries built a myth on the depravity of African women by misrepresenting three aspects of African/Shona customs.

First, explorers, settlers, and eventually both male and female missionaries described the marriage custom of Roora as a commercial exchange in which women are "bought" by men. Articles submitted to the home audience are replete with this imagery. This misrepresentation of Roora dated back to as early as the sixteenth century and continued throughout the colonial period. In his biography of Father Gonzalo Da Silveira, Chadwick explains that, after Chief Gamba of "Otongwe" accepted baptism in 1558, Silveira asked him to "separate himself from his extra wives, who as a pagan, he had seen fit to espouse." The chief's reluctance to accept this request to "put away his harem of women" stemmed from his awareness that with them lay "the hope of future wealth to be acquired by the barter of their female progeny."[31] Bourdillon cites another Portuguese source of this period that described the Roora marriage practice as a mere commercial exchange:

> It is a custom among the *kaffirs* for the husband to buy the wives from their parents. They agree upon a price and after it has been paid they

become relatives and are considered married. On the first day the bride and the groom go to their room and an old woman stays at the door until the bride says from the inside, "my husband is a man"; then the relatives outside celebrate with all kinds of drums and whistles.[32]

This interpretation of marriage customs was picked up by the nineteenth-century missionary church in southern Africa. Recall Bishop Hartzell's summary of the situation when he called wives slaves and their lives drudgery.

By creating and perpetuating such myths the church sought to show that evangelization was necessary for the abolishment of such "heathen" customs. By reducing the custom of Roora to a commercial enterprise that exchanged cattle for women, the church indirectly promoted the colonial schemes of the settler communities that alienated the Shona from their wealth in the form of herds of cattle.

Throughout the eighteenth and nineteenth centuries, settler communities in southern Africa raided and plundered the indigenous herds for personal use and ownership. A few historians have noted that it was the capital obtained from such cattle looting that ran the early colonial economies, such as the Cape Colony in South Africa. It is with this background that, for example, the Xhosa cattle killing of *Nonxause* should be studied. European early settlers, through the extermination of whole villages, warfare, tricks, and chicanery, sought to acquire all the cattle owned by the Africans. In southern Africa all these plunders and murders were justified by the settlers' argument that natives had no other plausible uses for cattle except for the "buying" of more wives into slavery. Dispossessing them of cattle was a swift method for liberating the women in the region.[33]

Ironically, after transferring ownership of land and cattle from African to European hands, the colonial government embarked on a new scheme of capitalizing on the myth of the Roora custom in its search for African labor. By the turn of the nineteenth century, indigenous herds in Zimbabwe had been depleted, the wars of resistance had been brutally quenched, and land had been apportioned for white ownership. The colonial state needed farm, domestic, and mining labor. The Shona and Ndebele communities had accepted their losses and were attempting to search for strategies for recovery and survival. Roora marriage customs were, for the second time, exploited and engineered to benefit the colonial state.

The state introduced what was termed "Customary Law," designed to govern "the natives." In this legal system the state recognized Roora custom as legitimate and made it mandatory for all "native" civil marriages. This meant that, upon marriage, each young man was to secure cattle or cash for the in-laws (which was not always so in Shona culture). Otherwise, the state or church would not recognize the marriage. With this law the colonial state lured landless and impoverished young men into bonded labor on farms and in mines to toil for money so that they could pursue the noble dream of "buying a wife" and settling down back in their village.

Beasts of Burden

In early missionary writings African women are portrayed as beasts of burden for their community. This myth caused the church to be largely silent while women were alienated from their fertile lands by colonial government. A classic example of such characterization is in an article submitted to the *Heathen Woman's Friend* in July 1899 by Erwin H. Richards, husband to Mrs. E. H. Richards. Entitled "Your Sister in Africa," the article characterizes the African woman as a purchased, degraded beast of burden. Accompanying the article is a picture of an elderly looking woman hoeing a seemingly dry patch. It reads:

> She is badly bent with her work; the devil will not allow her a handy-hoe with which she may stand up at work. He will not let her sons or her "owner" (she has no "husband") work in the field with her. [*Cf.* the Zulu article in the *Heathen Family News* above. *T.N.*]. She has no house. Her only clothing is a bit of bark from the body of a shrub. . . . There is a bit of femininity in her, and that is her ear-ring. This is pure and polished brass, and she is very proud of it. [Like most colonial sources in the region, Reverend Richards is aware of the fact but failed to note that these very women had been involved in global gold trade since the twelfth century. *T.N.*]. Her head is the freight train of the country. She is her husband's whole team, self-directing, self-loading. Self adjusting in all particulars, as her owner's. He bought her with

twenty pounds hard cash, or its equivalent. He may sell her whenever he fancies some other one, unless he has means to purchase the new without selling the old.[34]

Reverend Richards accurately portrayed the circumstances of the African woman in the dislocated African society at the turn of the century. In fact, it depicts the condition of the African woman in the whole southern African region after colonization. More than a decade earlier, Harry Agnew, co-missionary with Reverend Richards at Inhambane, gave a very different picture of the condition of the place and the people:

> The natives live chiefly by agriculture, each head of a family having a garden in which he cultivates corn, peanuts, cassava, pumpkin, sweet potatoes and so forth. Some also have plantations of coconut trees which bring them in a little revenue, although the products are sold so cheaply as to yield but little profit. Around the bay the men devote themselves to some extent catching fish, while the women gather up crabs and shellfish; so that, taking all things into consideration, there are no natives in South Africa [a term that included Zimbabwe *T.N.*] who live better than those of Inhambane.[35]

By 1899 around the Inhambane area the Portuguese and South African colonial system of coerced proletarization began to impact communities. In Mashonaland and Matebeleland the British had brutally but successfully stamped out the wars of resistance. In these areas the missions that seemed up to now to have labored in vain were being flooded by refugees so that some were even turned away. Unfortunately the mission in southern Africa did not admit or openly report to the church back home that its early converts were predominantly political refugees. The church acquired land and created Christian villages for these "converts." *Makhorwa* ("the saved ones") was born.

Having stayed in this part of the Continent for almost twenty years, Reverend Richards had seen the change of the landscape, as the colonially induced cultural transformation was taking its effect on communities in the region. By 1900, proxy wars, cattle raiding, land annexation policies, and the uprooting of whole communities were the order of the day in the region. The gold and diamond industrial economy was beginning to dictate the policies to whites in South Africa, as well as to the adjoining territories. By distorting the facts of the condition of the African woman prior to colonialism, the early missionaries secured a mandate for continuing missionary activity and beginning women's work among the Africans. By so doing, the mission church would also advance the colonial course in the name of "civilizing the natives."

In turn, the colonial process was the machine that churned out the mythical portrait of an African woman as a totally depraved creature. The colonial farming and industrial economy had been designed to leave the African woman with no land, property, male labor, and spouse, since the men left for the farms and industrial centers in search of survival. The myth of the African male as lazy and shiftless also served to justify alienating males so that they would become laborers for the colonial machine.[36] In this new environment the young men would quickly adopt the master's language of a capitalist economy in which all modes of exchange involving currency are perceived as commercial commodity. The custom of Roora came to be viewed as a commercial transaction in which a young man "bought" a woman for the purposes of reproduction and production.

My mother remembers the day and the process that disrupted and dispossessed her community of the Mapara people forever. On this day they were to be forcibly repatriated from their homeland, Nyanhundu—the land where she was born and raised and where her people had lived for generations. The land literally flowed with milk and honey, she said. In 1947, this paradise was suddenly lost when trucks from the Rhodesia government arrived to repatriate the entire community to Nyautare, a place eighty miles northeast of Nyanhundu. This forced repatriation exercise followed soon after a brief notification from the government, leaving no time for resistance.

Other Voices

At the turn of the century, other voices (but only a few early missionary women and men) gave an accurate picture of the condition of indigenous women and men in Africa. John White and Arthur Shearly Cripps of Mashonaland underscored the beauty and strength of Shona culture. From the beginning to the end of their work among the Shona, these two would openly defend and protect indigenous customs from colonial assault. Despite stern opposition, resentment, and open hostility, not just from the colonial community but also from the church, the two men would speak the truth as they saw it. For example, on the myths of the laziness of the Shona male and the drudgery of the Shona female, Steere cites Shearly Cripps, who wrote home to caution, "When you read philanthropic and disinterested mine-owners' lamentations over the good-for-nothing laziness of kaffir mankind and the joyless drudgery of kaffir woman-kind, please be faithless and unbelieving."

In their own limited way, the first two bishops of the Anglican Church in Zimbabwe, Knight George Bruce and William Thomas Gaul, tried to acknowledge the strengths of Shona culture. Despite his colonial bias against the Shona and Ndebele pre-colonial relations in 1890, when writing to his Provincial Synod, Bishop Bruce wrote:

> It must not be forgotten that the Mashona people are a nation of slaves, and they inherited the unusual characteristics of slaves. With all their faults, they are a pleasanter people to deal with than the Matebele. They are gentle, industrious, and skillful, but they are cut off, man, woman, and child, with no chance of escape and no hope of succor. Their slaughter by the Matebele goes on . . . .[37]

Farrant further cites an interview in 1898 in which Bishop Gaul, in his own manner, firmly disagrees with the colonial mythical image of the lazy Shona.

John White and Shearly Cripps not only chose to highlight the good within Shona culture but, as early missionaries, also elected to struggle and identify totally with the suffering and pain of a people being colonized. For example, during the 1896 Shona war of resistance John White played the role of intermediary between the colonial government and the Chiremba people of Epworth Farm. To prove loyalty to them, White would sleep among them outside the European laager as an assurance that the whites would not kill them.

White is quoted to have said to them, "I will sleep each night among you, outside the laager, so that if they come to kill you, they will kill me also."[38]

Writing much later in 1938 on the custom of Roora, Charlotte Wright, wife of the bishop of the African Methodist Episcopal Church in South Africa, argues that the totality of the marriage process in African societies is very self-affirming for young women. Her understanding of the custom is summed up thusly, "*Lobola* is really a form of marriage dowry; however, instead of being settled on the bride by her parents, it is settled on the bride's family by the bridegroom or his family, and it means that the bride may return to her family and be ungrudgingly cared for in the case of misfortune or ill-treatment."[39]

In the early phase of their ministry in the native church, American Protestant women missionaries enjoyed historic freedoms in early colonial southern Africa. In these early years, Mrs. Rasmussen at Old Mutare was involved in almost all areas of the founding of the mission among the Manyika. She translated texts, headed school, traveled, preached, and taught school.

However, in this frontier context the church and settler community forged a symbiotic relationship in which usually the mission of the one was indistinguishable from that of the other. Pioneer church leaders like Anglican bishop Knight Bruce questioned this "unholy alliance" between the early missionary church and the colonial state in what later became Rhodesia.[40] Arthur Shearly Cripps would totally reject this relationship and eventually opt to disassociate himself from the Anglican Church, but he continued to minister in its parish at Maronda Mashanu. In such a context, the church embarked on its mission with a blurred vision.

Most of the early women missionaries fell victim to colonial myths and propaganda. Their ministry among women such as the Manyika was designed to address areas that the colonial authorities claimed to have identified as problematic within these communities. Also, the church generally accepted the colonial blueprint for indigenous societies, designed to justify the exploitation or assault of every aspect of a people's existence. After the church bought into the colonial myth of portraying Manyika women as a powerless, miserable lot, its mission would barely meet their needs. With the help of the colonial state, the early church's civilizing mission to Manyika women would coerce them into the limited Victorian space of the domestic sphere.

The church's mission among African women implicitly endorsed the processes that alienated them from their land and made them exchange a hoe for a broom. When the church campaigned to liberate Manyika women from drudgery, it was also bringing to an end the women's role of co-provider—a role they took very seriously. Through mission education, the first Manyika women experienced the world of Christianity under a racist colonialism. It was resistance to this racist colonialism that led the early Manyika women converts to found Rukwadzano as a movement and organization.

CHAPTER 3

Colonialism and the Bible: Forced Renunciations

THIS CHAPTER SEEKS TO HIGHLIGHT TWO THEMES IN THE INTRODUCTION OF Christianity to African women by early missionary women in southern Africa. First, I show that early missionary women were architects and co-founders of the early Christian communities that would develop the Christian church in the region. In the Methodist Episcopal Church at Old Mutare, Zimbabwe, a response and initiative of the African women to these early efforts by women missionaries were the birth of the Rukwadzano movement/organization in 1938. Second, I show that the effects of colonialism and racism were so pervasive that they undeniably undermined the mission and message of the church, as given in the Christian gospel, at every juncture in southern Africa. Some early women missionaries apparently struggled between the irreconcilable worldviews of the Bible and that of European colonialism in southern Africa. But a majority of the early missionary women had no problem with totally rejecting the African worldview.

One can argue that it was not the bureaucracy of the women's missionary societies back in the United States that stifled women's support for overseas missions in southern Africa but rather a missionary church that could no longer continue to pretend to be impartial on issues of race and colonialism. After World War II, when the global discourse had shifted toward defense of justice, human rights, and self-rule for colonized peoples, southern Africa was drafting and instituting draconian laws intended to reinforce colonialism and white supremacy. In such an environment, the church's efforts at educating African women paradoxically seemed to help perpetuate the white colonial state. The church would educate and train girls into limited professional areas designated by the colonial state for black women only. The curriculum and environment in which these women were educated and socialized were becoming more and more hierarchical along the lines of gender and race.

In One's Own Image

Early women missionaries generally defined their mission among African women as one of rescuing them from what they perceived as the three "evils" that victimized them: polygamy, Roora, and drudgery. After conversion the single solution to these evils was to prepare them for "Christian marriage." Missionary views on Christian marriage as a cure-all to native women's problems are well captured by an article in the February 1870 issue of the *Heathen Woman's Friend.* The writer characterizes a woman's conversion to Christianity as the most rational of decisions because, she contends, in Christianity she is most secure in marriage. According to her, a Christian marriage is a woman's 'Magna Charta'" in that her rights and privileges are protected. The author expounds further:

> The sacredness of marriage is one of its principles. Understanding this, women should hold unyieldingly to the religion of the Bible. They should guard the sanctity of the marriage relation as they would the title deed to their homes, the right to their own children.[1]

With this general conviction the early missionary women would design the first curriculum for the first Manyika young women converts. The first generation of young women to come to the mission center at Old Mutare, as was the case with many other early mission centers in the region, would be prepared as candidates for marriage to the young pastors being trained at the mission. These young women would be fashioned in the image of the early missionary women as wives, mothers, and preachers. It was out of these early African women converts that Rukwadzano would be born and officially organized at Old Mutare in 1938.

As Refugees

For almost five years, as a missionary sent by the Methodist Episcopal Church Women's Foreign Missionary Society to work with Manyika women at Old Mutare, Mrs. Helen Rasmussen had labored in vain. She had failed to secure any young girls who would voluntarily come to the mission. In reporting her difficulty she noted further that she had considered abandoning the mission as a logical option; but encouragement from Bishop Hartzell caused her to decide to stay. The situation baffled her: precisely in the land Cecil Rhodes especially favored for the founding of a new empire, everything seemed to discourage the establishment of God's kingdom.[2]

A major break came in 1905 when Gumba, one of the chief's daughters, and a number of other girls turned up at the mission and asked Mrs. Helen Rasmussen to teach them to read and write. Within a decade girls had so flooded the school that some had to be turned away. The early women missionaries gave no explanation as to why the tide had turned so suddenly.[3] Gumba and her colleagues were the group out of which the Methodist Episcopal Church would secure its first converts among the Manyika. These girls were political refugees, casualties of the colonial schemes of dispossession.

Five years earlier Shakeni had been the first Manyika young woman sent to the mission. Shakeni's mother sent her to Mrs. Rasmussen after her mother and Mrs. Rasmussen had become friends.

Individuals like Shakeni, who were actually marginalized in their indigenous societies, were the first to find their way to the mission and become part of the early church in southern Africa. Such individuals would have included the socially stigmatized, the poor, the companionless, and the abused. It was this phenomenon that spurred the myth among the early missionary women, the church, and colonial literature that every girl coming to the mission was a social refugee. All of the girls who came to the mission in this early period in southern Africa were portrayed as runaways or social refugees who were fleeing from drudgery or from being sold in marriage to polygamous old men. In a chapter entitled "Sweet Sixteen" from her book, Rasmussen highlights this theme as follows:

> Sweet Sixteen also likes the boys after the most approved fashion. She wants to marry one of these handsome young fellows. And who can blame her? They are to be preferred to the dirty old heathen in the kraal, to whom she likely already had been sold by her parents. Most likely she fled to the mission as to the city as a refuge to escape being forced into such a marriage.[4]

Early missionaries in southern Africa neglected to point out that a majority of the young people, including women like Gumba, in fact came to the mission as political refugees. In Mashonaland and Matebeleland the Africans had conceded power to the British colonial authorities after losing the 1896 war of resistance. During this period, the Methodist Episcopal Church came into the region through the agency of Bishop Hartzell, who met with Cecil John Rhodes and was given land and property at Old Mutare on condition that the church would open a school for the education of white children in Mutare. In this 1897 meeting with Rhodes in London, the bishop shared his ambitions for Africa; and Mr. Rhodes in turn presented his as "[m]y greatest ambition is two fold: to do the greatest possible thing for barbaric humanity, and to do all in my power to promote the unity of the English-speaking races of the world. When the unity is a fact there will be no more war."[5]

The bishop's support for the colonization of Africa was unwavering and is reflected in his writing. For example, he felt that the Berlin Conference of 1885 marked the beginning of a new era for Africa. He wrote, "For the advance of the missionary, as well as the explorer, law and order were necessary. Under the providence of God this was accomplished by the partition of the continent."[6]

Throughout the nineteenth and the early twentieth centuries the Methodist Episcopal Church in the United States would blindly support the colonization of Africa. One of the explanations for this support was that such an undertaking would be an effective means of abolishing the slave trade on the continent. (In this context the slave trade was generally depicted as mainly an Arab/Muslim enterprise.) The colonization and partition of Africa were heralded as an approach that would finally open up the continent for legitimate trade. American Methodists would greet the arrival of The Pioneer Column, led by Cecil John Rhodes, into Mashonaland as a great accomplishment leading toward this objective. Under the title "The El Dorado of Africa" an article in Bishop Taylor's magazine, *Africa News*, explains:

> Not a drop of blood was spilt during this expedition and "the natives of Mashonaland have hailed the advent of the whites as the dawn of a blessed era in which they have been rescued from the Matebele who have raided their country, killed them indiscriminately, and carry their wives and children into slavery." Mashonaland is depicted as the Eldorado of Africa because it is said to be finely adapted both to grazing and agriculture, and, under the influence of the plow and scythe, explorers report that it can be made to teem with agricultural blessings, and become the happy home of thousands of European farmers.... But this is not all. If reports are to be believed, not even the splendid gold fields of the South African republic compare with the riches that are in store for the miners who are now following the footsteps of the first expedition in Mashonaland.

The article proceeds to explain how the policies of the Company are designed as to ensure the welfare of the native people. These articles were propagandistic in favor of white colonization and never really told the home audience the truth as to the experiences of the native peoples.[7]

The Settler Church

At the official opening of the first Annual Conference of the East Central Africa Conference of the Methodist Episcopal Church in 1901, Bishop Hartzell was given as a gift a gavel made from the butt of a gun used in the failed war of resistance (1895–97) for opening and officiating at the Conference. It was also at this Conference that the minutes allude to but do not elaborate on the pressing "Native Question" as it was called by both the early church and the colonial government. The "Native Question" simply focused on what to do with the defeated natives. This is a dramatic beginning for the church because, with its official opening, it was also celebrating the colonial triumph in the territory. Yet the unforeseen 1896 war of resistance robbed both the church and the colony of complacency. In this war mission centers were targets and missionaries were killed. For example, Bernard Mizeki of the Anglican Church had been murdered at Mangwende, and so had Moleli and others of the Wesleyan Methodist Church at Nengubo.[8]

The British South Africa Company granted the Methodist Episcopal Church 13,000 acres at Old Mutare. The Company claimed it had paid $100,000 to the newly established colonial government for the land. The Methodist Episcopal Church showed no reservation in circumventing the indigenous authorities and recognizing the British as the legitimate owners of the land. The church wanted sites for missions and a guarantee for protection, and the colonial powers needed a religious mandate for their "mission." The Methodist Episcopal Church of this period never resolved the "Native Question." Instead it silently watched from the citadels of its colonially granted mission lands as all fertile lands were taken for European settlement and the natives were marched off to reservations designed to create reservoirs for settler labor markets.[9]

The process of land acquisition by the missionary church in Zimbabwe created an unresolved ethical dilemma that has persisted: who owned the land? Was the church going to honor and recognize the native claims to ownership of land and therefore seek their permission to build a mission in a particular place? Or was it going to honor and recognize the British colonial government's claims to ownership of land instead? The church chose the latter option because it politically guaranteed two vital interests. First, the church would almost be guaranteed permission to build on any site of its choice without much negotiation by the colonial government. Second, as long as the colonial government prevailed, the church would be guaranteed protection and the right to stay.

This dilemma was debated poignantly by Anglican Bishop Knight Bruce in his book *Memories of Mashonaland*. Bishop Bruce explains that during this early period, despite native claims, the church adopted the colonial rationale that all uninhabited land belonged to nobody and therefore was available for acquisition.[10] In this situation all the church needed to do to secure land was to map out a desired territory or site and fill out an application form for company approval. By 1897, the Church of England had acquired twenty-five tracts of land comprised of three-thousand acres each. Bishop Bruce then proceeded to question the necessity of an alliance between the church and a colonial government. He argued that it was possible for the church to deal directly with the native peoples on the issue of land.

Bruce cites an example of the American Board mission at Melsetter, south of Manyikaland, in which the church had successfully negotiated with native peoples and been granted permission to found a mission. However, such an arrangement was unacceptable to both the church and the colonial powers. For the church, the recognition of native peoples as the legitimate owners of the land caused great anxiety because such a situation usually called for a tedious process of negotiation. And afterward, there was no guarantee of a permanent settlement for the church. On the other hand, colonialists and settlers like Cecil Rhodes were desperately in search of a religious endorsement to their "mission" for Africa. The church's recognition of native people as the legitimate owners of land would have been viewed by colonialists as a blatantly hostile move.

In an attempt to absolve the church of involvement in such an "unholy alliance," some church leaders, like Knight Bruce, quickly revised their opinion on the ethics of land acquisition by the church. As the tentacles of colonization grabbed one territory after another, these leaders justified the church's involvement by saying that the church was finding a way of securing "reserves" of land for future use in case native people ran out of land. Bishop Bruce was even uncertain as to what term one could comfortably use for these "pieces" of land. His was a futile attempt to project an image of the church that was divorced from the colonial establishment. He ultimately and reluctantly accepted the term *farm* as used by the British South Africa Company to describe the pieces of land taken by the church. Toward the end of his book, the bishop makes his peace with this dilemma. The church, he says, deserves these lands as a reward for the "sweat of our brow," in that all the earlier sacrifices and frustrating endeavors to founding missions were finally being rewarded.[11]

Educating a Conquered Woman

The girls who came to the mission in 1904 were political refugees. Gumba and her colleagues were members of a defeated people. By this time both the Shona and the Ndebele were beginning to accept that the mission and the missionaries were there to stay. In the war of resistance the mission and its missionaries had been targeted for destruction as agents of white colonization. Black missionaries, like Bernard Mizeki of the Anglican Church at Mangwende and M. Moleli of the Wesleyan Methodist Church at Nengubo, had been killed as colonialist collaborators.[12] After the dust settled, the church picked up on its mission and continued to define it as that of saving the Manyika from heathenism. In this post-colonization era the church further defined its mission to include teaching European culture and civilization, a subject it considered suitable only for those of the Christian religion.

Having rejected the Shona worldview, the church continued to struggle to reconcile the worldviews of the Bible, on the one hand, and European racial, industrial capitalism, on the other. For example, Bishop Hartzell defined the second primary purpose of the mission center at Old Mutare (apart from evangelism) as that of becoming an industrial center where young people would be trained in what he called "Christian industrial education." Christian industrial education, he said, "transforms the native from a lazy, superstitious heathen into a skilled Christian workman."[13] At this juncture the church's mission overlapped with the colonialist dream. In both cases they were intended to transform the local economic system from an agrarian to a capitalist industrialist system. Even Mrs. Rasmussen echoes this dream when she reports back home, "The mountains that surround us are veined with gold, and already only seven miles away there are two mines running full blast, day and night, and the percentage of gold to the ton is really greater than at Johannesburg."[14]

In her selective reporting she fails to mention that the Manyika had, in their own way, traded in gold from these mines for over five-hundred years or that the labor being used to keep the mines running full blast, day and night, was effectively compulsory. This was the beginning of an economic system that would tear the Manyika family apart as the men were drafted into compulsory labor.[15] This migrant-labor system would intensify and escalate as the colonial economy deeply entrenched itself among the Manyika and in the region. Men would supply labor in the mines and farms for indefinite periods of time as collateral for the government-imposed hut, or head, tax. Failure to comply resulted in imprisonment.

There was one missionary, Shearly Cripps, who was truthful about the situation of the Shona women and the nature of work needed among them. According to Steere, Cripps had long felt the need for women workers at his mission and constantly shared this with the Synod. Cripps did not portray the mission of these workers as one of rescuing Shona women from the evils of a heathen culture. For Cripps, white women workers were needed because

> the girls and women had no one to help in the intimate womanly way that is so necessary to form them [women converts] in the Christian life, and to share their family problems. All of this need had been so accentuated among the Mashona people by their being compelled to face the intrusions of the new white rulers of the country, and their ways of organizing the productive economy of the territory, which so often robbed them of their men folk for long periods at a time. Such white women could do much in the schools.[16]

Cripps confesses frankly that many a death among his small company of Christian Africans might have been avoided if a trained woman worker's vigilant care had been given early enough.[17]

On mission lands the church decided to create social laboratories from which new converts were spawned and commissioned to outer stations, where they were expected to duplicate the process. At the mission the new converts would learn both the fundamentals of the new religion and the skills for living out the new lifestyle. When young people came to the mission, they joined a community they were expected to associate with for the rest of their lives. The mission was being designed not just to accommodate students but also to serve as permanent settlement for the newly married couples. These young couples would form the nucleus of the new Christian community, known as *Makhorwa*, "the saved ones." The outstations were expected to duplicate this design as well.

The Boarding School

The first group of Manyika girls who arrived at the mission in 1904 moved into the "Villa," the women's dormitory, and were expected to leave for home visits only during the holidays. Such visits were eventually curtailed because some girls allegedly never came back. Upon arriving at the mission, the young women would be introduced to a well-designed curriculum and a plan for how they would receive training. The rationale behind creating mission boarding schools for children and youth was based on two general beliefs. First, young people made the best candidates for both religious and industrial training because they were "malleable." Second, confining the young or converts to a mission environment until graduation severed them from the contamination of "heathen influences" in the village from which they came.

In southern Africa boarding schools and the mission would become halfway houses where the young were "processed," or "groomed," for leadership in the new era of a Christian civilization. Most of the missionaries at the mission in this early period tenaciously held the view that European culture or civilization was the only appropriate medium through which Christianity could be effectively communicated and lived. Even the Reverend John White of the Wesleyan Methodist Church argued the two were inseparable: "Civilization without Christianity is a doubtful gift. Education, without the restraints and discipline of the Christian faith, may be a danger rather than a boon to these heathen people," he argued.[18]

Thus, the boarding school became the place for teaching the European worldview along with the new religion. It is important to note that in Zimbabwe, this missionary view of teaching Africans

European culture was not popular with the European settlers in the region. Colonial settlers viewed the missionary task of "civilizing" the natives as outright dangerous to settler survival.[19] The settlers felt that by "civilizing" the natives, the missionaries were actually creating a class of Africans that would eventually rise up and demand civil and political rights.

> The real issue here between the church and state centered on who had the power to determine the destiny of the Africans who had become a conquered people. The church was convinced it could create a new breed of Africans who would be both devout Christians and citizens of a new industrial society, who would obey civil authority, and at some point would participate in matters of state government. The state was suspicious of the church's religious doctrine and its effects on the Africans, as well as the church's proposed curriculum to "civilize" the Africans because it feared it might succeed in creating independent leaders.[20]

The church and state never got ample time to resolve this controversy. Due to anxiety and uncertainty in the villages, large numbers of dislocated young Africans flocked to the mission, creating a crisis for the mission budget. The state offered to bail out the church, offering the mission school grants on condition that the state have a say in drafting the curriculum for "native education" taught in mission schools. According to Miss Sophia Jordan Coffin, who officially took over mission work among the Manyika girls in 1907 after Mrs. Rasmussen's marriage, the government offered them funds only on condition that they have "Domestic Work" in their curriculum.

Faced with a budget crisis, yet fired by the zeal for mass recruitment, most churches accepted the colonial government's offer, fully aware of the strings attached. Missionaries like Shearly Cripps vehemently protested this *quid pro quo* arrangement between church and state. He accused the Zimbabwean missionary churches (all denominations) of being driven by the ambitions of building the institutional church or empire rather than a church in the hearts and minds of the Shona and Ndebele people. Cripps viewed these government schemes as evil plots of entrapment. For him, the church's decision to accept government funding was another act of ultimate betrayal of the African quest for self-determination. Cripps argued that the church's decision to feed from the colonial government's hand meant it had again become an agent in the enslavement of a people.[21]

At the mission center the Manyika children encountered a world that required them to renounce all that pertained to their family and heritage. Indigenous arts, science, religion, and philosophy were dismissed as pagan. Ironically, in this zeal to propagate a civilized Christianity, the church also introduced two conflicting worldviews to the young women and men. On the one hand, there was the biblical worldview that it sought to communicate to the new converts. On the other hand, it also held to a Euro-American culture/civilization that was seeking to divorce itself from all matters of religion via the scientific method.[22] The colonial state's interest in securing the right to draft the nature and content of mission-education curriculum served to ensure that the church would communicate as legitimate not only the biblical worldview but also the Western worldview.

This conflicting yet symbiotic relationship between the church and state on matters of educating the young Africans became a symbol of the struggle between missionary and colonial settler. As time went on this situation would gradually inflict immense damage on the psyche of the African child. During the early colonial period, the church shaped the young African mind with a biblical worldview that rejected indigenous culture and accepted the fundamentals of Western culture as Christian.

In this formative period up to the 1940s mission graduates were articulate in the biblical worldview and some were even bold enough to seek to appropriate it for indigenous culture. This was the group that formed the nucleus of the Rukwadzano movement and of the independent churches. In the later colonial period the government's grip on African education tightened, and the emphasis on the curriculum shifted toward the Western scientific worldview. The bedrock of this worldview consisted of rigid hierarchies on issues of race, gender, class, and the environment.[23] The church of this period directed its energy toward further institutional expansion and issues of ecclesiastical orthodoxy in polity and doctrine.

Manyika Girls at the Mission

Early missionary women at Old Mutare designed an education for young girls based on the myth that they were runaways fleeing from a hideous culture. Upon arrival at the mission a young woman was usually given soap and water, a "proper" dress, and finally a Christian name.

Young girls who came to the mission during this period were not earmarked for industrial or ministerial training as were the boys. Instead, the young women would be trained for leadership that mirrored the early missionary woman's own image. They were going to be trained to become what the women's missionary society defined as examples of "respectable womanhood."

In this context the young women would be trained to become wives and mothers, as well as partners in ministry with their Christian husbands. The Bible would be introduced as the primary text from which they were taught to read and write for eventual purposes of evangelism. The women's curriculum used soap to train the young women to seek the status of "elevated womanhood" through "hygiene." Soap symbolized a women's initiation into a "civilization" that associated women with hygiene and cleanliness. With soap and broom young women were expected to create model homes and families that would be called "Christian." By 1906 this experiment had proved to be quite successful because, after making a visit to her former students' "kraal," Miss Jordan Coffin reports:

> It was interesting to see their homes and note improvement in their manner of living. They eat from tables, have white tablecloths and suitable dishes. They have civilized beds, and flowers in every conceivable place. Our chief object is to train these girls for Christian homes and instill in them an earnest desire to spread the Gospel among their own people.[24]

In this training of the Manyika woman the Methodist Episcopal Church had embarked on a revolutionary social project. The Manyika women who became Christians would come out on the lowest rung on the totem pole of a Christian, civilized village. In this village the woman was viewed as having been rescued from the dirt and grime of outdoor work into the domestic sphere, where she could be groomed into a "Victorian lady" of the house. A Victorian model of ideal womanhood would be superimposed on the Manyika woman by the church.

By abandoning their piece of land to men and to the colonialists, Christianized African women became terminally economically crippled. They surrendered all their economic power to their husbands. The church socialized these Christianized women to stay in the house and use soap to make themselves and the house acceptable for their husbands.[25] The church indirectly helped the colonial state in two critical areas. By domesticating Manyika women, the church eliminated competition on the job market by creating jobs only for men. Moreover, in training women for a civilized lifestyle, the church was creating a consumer class that would boost the new colonial economy.

Bible Women

The curriculum for the early phase of training for the young women focused on religious education accompanied by domestic work. Unlike later groups, who would receive an education for professional training, these first young women, as Bible women, though subservient, would in their own way be trained to assume leadership in the new community. As wives of evangelists, they had to receive special training, after which they would assume special responsibilities. During this introductory training phase Manyika women acquired three fundamental elements as Bible women. First, they were introduced to two new worldviews, that of the Bible and that of the Europeans. Second, they were initiated into the world of literacy; they acquired the skills of reading and writing. And third, after this training, they were given the authority to preach and lead other women in the church.

By 1901 Mrs. Springer (formerly Mrs. Rasmussen), having learned the fundamentals of the Manyika language, had started on the translations of the scriptures and other materials for use by the mission. Through this literature she would introduce Manyika women to the world of the Bible. The education of these women introduced them to a new worldview, a new religion. They were expected gradually to absorb the fundamentals of this new religion and, as soon as possible, take it to their own women back in the village. Within this evangelical tradition some women seized the opportunity for the application of a hermeneutic based on their personal experiences in the new faith. Knowledge of the biblical worldview formed the bedrock upon which these women would base their faith in the movement/organization they founded in 1929.

Early missionary women drilled the young women in stories and readings from the Bible and the church. Even before some of the girls committed themselves to coming to stay at the mission, Mrs. Springer would entice them with the pictures and stories of the new religion. Explaining how she enticed Mukonyerwa to school, she writes:

> By this time the girls had cleaned up considerably and I enjoyed their company and missed them when they were gone. Evening after evening they would come into the study as soon as their supper was eaten, sit down on the floor near my feet and say, "Missisi, won't you show us some pictures?" And then I would get out some Sunday School cards or the like and tell them stories until I was completely talked out. I shall never forget the keen, intense interest of these two girls as they listened night after night to this same story... But it was four years before Mukonyerwa came to us and said she wanted to stay and attend the school. I was very ill in bed but when they told me that she had come, I rejoiced greatly. She had another girl with her.[26]

These young women would be expected to renounce totally their own culture and to look forward to marrying the young men at the mission. The girls proceeded to learn reading and writing. The power of literacy not only enabled them to read the Bible stories by themselves but also equipped them with a fundamental tool for keeping up with events of the colonial experience. Mrs. Springer again summarizes well the basic tasks, besides singing and praying, set for the girls to learn:

> But oh! how much there is for her to learn! To be prompt, and quick and clean and truthful! To learn the value of time! All her teachers need infinite patience on that score! . . . She learns to read and write with remarkable rapidity. A few months' lessons with the needle will enable

her to excel many an American girl of her age. For Sweet Sixteen's sewing lessons are practical dressmaking, darning, mending and fine needlework.[27]

The early missionary women never missed the primary objective of recruiting young women to the mission. The young girls were at the mission so that in two or three years they would have a Christian wedding and go out with "her husband to win the other girls and women to the Master whom she has come to know and serve." In the new worldview the women came to learn of a God who was a "Master," but a loving one. In this world women's status was a little lower than that of men because they could not achieve the same status in leadership. Furthermore, while intolerant of indigenous culture, this world was quite open to European culture. European culture or civilization in this context was expressed by the conquering spirit that sought to tame and exploit native peoples, animals, and the environment.

The early missionary women to southern African fostered the development of the mission school. However, these missionaries were unable to mute the negative effects of colonialism and racism. In fact, the colonial allegiance took precedence over the religious undertaking of the women in the mission schools; and colonialism also subverted the biblical message. When it came to choosing between the faith taught by Christianity and that practiced by non-African missionaries, the missionaries always sided with colonial forces rather than the gospel. Moreover, the worldview that shaped Africans prior to colonialism was rejected by the missionaries, and mission girls were urged to leave their culture behind.

CHAPTER 4

Teaching Renunciation of Shona Culture

THIS CHAPTER CONTINUES THE DISCUSSION EXPLORED IN THE PREVIOUS chapter relating to the efforts of the missionaries to teach the rejection of Shona culture. The focus here is on the curriculum taught by missionaries and their efforts to use the mission school to teach a curriculum of cultural renunciation.

The mission boarding school taught the girls concepts and etiquette in areas such as dress, courtship, marriage, or motherhood. Almost all of these new forms of behavior were drawn from the Euro-American pattern that did not always reconcile well with the biblical pattern. The boarding school became the social arena where young women would be coerced to learn European culture as the only model acceptable and compatible with the Christian religion.

The Politics of Soap

Soap was a symbol of the acculturation or the process through which young women underwent alienation from their culture. It was also symbolic of the focal point on which the missionary and the colonialist agreed as the point of departure for the "civilizing of the native." At the first encounter with the Shona or Ndebele, both the missionary and the settler expressed utter repugnance at what they named as African lack of personal hygiene. The Africans were always described at first sight as filthy, smelly creatures living in depraved and deplorable conditions. Indigenous female and male beauty or cosmetic styles, such as the use of red ochre or animal fat on the "black" face and body, were cast as filthy and gross. Missionary as well as colonial literature of the period highlighted and colored these habits to create an image of the "otherness" of the Africans.

The white settlers regarded soap as the answer to the depraved condition of the native. It was the magic that could at least get rid of the filth and groom him or her for use in domestic labor. In the eyes of the settler, soap, however, would never wash away the "blackness" of the native skin to elevate them to the intellectual and social status of the whites. In the colonial world the adjectives used to describe the condition of the Africans, such as *filthiness* and *darkness*, were also racial metaphors meant to represent the color black. Juxtaposed to these metaphors were other adjectives, such as *primitive*, *savage*, *ignorant* or *depraved*, that further served to convey the idea that the condition of the Africans was terminally inferior, both physically and mentally.[1] Colonial circles believed soap would at least clean them up enough so that they could be employed, but it would never wash away their "blackness."

Whiteness, on the other hand, represented all that was desirable in the colonial world. In this world whiteness was a metaphor not just for cleanliness but also for a superior civilization. The word *white* always occurred contiguously with words such as *people*, *beauty*, *civil*, *order*, *intelligence*, and *history*. The colonial world was rigid, hierarchical, and dualistic. All reality was constructed to ensure the perpetuation of white male hegemony in all matters of existence. This colonial world was ordered along gender, race, species, and class hierarchies.

At the mission, soap symbolized the rite of passage into the world of a civilization that the mission church put forth as normative. The use of soap was almost mandatory at the mission. A person's agreement to use soap for bathing seemed to symbolize renunciation of or shedding off the "native-self."

Like their colonial counterparts early missionaries described the "blackness" of Africans in a metaphorical way that cast them as a "cursed race." Early missionary literature is replete with adjectives like *savage*, *heathen*, *pagan*, *filthy*, and *dark* to convey the "otherness" of the Africans as compared with Europeans. When early missionaries referred to themselves as "us," one always had to discern whether the term meant race or religion. Generally it meant both.

The mission church believed that soap had the power to wash the outer shell of the Shona and Ndebele until it became, if not white, then at least as clean as that of the white man. The church, however, went further and preached that the gospel could cleanse and enlighten the inner self of the Africans and thus make racial equality an attainable goal. It was around this belief that the colonial state would view the missionary church with a perpetual eye of suspicious paranoia. Churches or individual missionaries who openly espoused ideas of racial equality were not immune from secret government monitoring or surveillance.

At the mission center girls traded their traditional hairstyles and cosmetic paraphernalia for European-looking ones. Here images of outward beauty continued to be associated with the color white. Colonial media and propaganda portrayed one's skin-color shade as the primary physical attribute for judging beauty and character. Gradually it would become acceptable, even preferable, among the Shona to be light skinned.

Prior to this colonial experience, light-skinned individuals were discreetly discriminated against in Shona culture. Such sayings as *"Munhu mutsvuku akasaba anoroya"* ("A light-skinned person is either a thief or a witch") were not uncommon among the Shona. There was even the belief that light-skinned persons attracted lightening! Such sayings may have appeared in Shona worldview after the people's encounter with a light-skinned people who were dishonest. The Shona had such historic encounters with both the Arabs and the Portuguese before colonization.[2]

On the subject of dishonesty, it was a popular sport within both the church and the colony to paint Africans as inherently liars and thieves. In 1903 Mrs. Rasmussen traveled on the newly completed railway to Bulawayo for the official dedication of a Methodist Episcopal church. On that occasion she came across a Reverend Mr. Helm, a veteran missionary who had worked in that region for thirty years. As they were reminiscing and celebrating the gospel influence, he recalled "the early years when truth and honesty were unknown and murder the common order of the day. Thieving was punishable with death; yet everyone stole, stole anything, anywhere." Mrs. Rasmussen in turn marveled at the influence of the gospel by highlighting that "nearly a thousand natives had swarmed the grounds, having access to all parts of the house and grounds, not a penny's worth disappeared."[3]

Dress

Young women also changed their style of dress at the mission. Simple styles of Shona women's dress of bare head and shoulders, cloth-wrap, jewelry, and other ornaments would be traded in for a covered head, an elaborately sewn Victorian dress, no make-up, and minimal jewelry and ornaments. The mission church perceived the trading of dressing and cosmetic style from indigenous to Euro-American as a convert's statement of renunciation of the old and embracing the new. On this subject Mrs. Rasmussen, who was not very enthusiastic about adoption of European style of dress by the girls at Old Mutare, writes:

> I used to regret the tendency of the girls to get at once into European clothes. Clothed they surely needed to be but it seemed to me this could better be accomplished by some oriental style of dress more hygienic than our occidental one. . . . I think now that the existing circumstances and the contact the Africans have with white women, not only justify but commend a European style of clothing. One bright, highly educated young woman of another part of Africa said that she had never known a mission girl to go back to heathenism as long as she wore her foreign clothing. But if she lapsed, the first sign of it was a return to the native garment or loin cloth.[4]

Sexuality

Coming out of the Victorian culture, the mission church from its beginning registered strong sentiments of disapproval toward all forms of African sexuality. The mission church regarded African openness to the subject of sexuality with shock and suspicion. In reaction, missionaries created a myth in which all of African culture and thought were allegedly fixated on sexuality. In her book *I Married a Missionary*, Zelma Lawyer explains this myth succinctly:

The pre-adolescent boys and girls are not taught by their parents that intercourse between the sexes is taboo. Rather the practice is encouraged as a preparation for adult life, the whole of which revolves around sex, the one predominating and ruling element of all Native life. Its importance, its necessity, its gravity, is as great as that of eating or drinking or sleeping. It is on the same level. There are no virgins among the natives. When I asked our language teacher the Tonga word for "virgin," he said, "There is none." . . . After adolescence, however, a mighty effort is made to keep the fond youngsters apart. But of course it's too late. They're as hard to control as some white boys and girls I have heard of.[5]

By reducing all of African experience to sexuality, this myth was also meant to show that the Africans were anthropologically inferior to other races because they had been incapable of constructing a system of religious or scientific thought. They were therefore lowest on the "totem pole" of the evolution process. In this context the missionary task was understood as that of developing the African mind to rational capacity. Such a judgment of African culture again reflected the missionary church's dualistic worldview, which considered the body and the mind as separate entities in perpetual struggle for dominance.[6]

In this worldview, the body, or the physical, represented the base, lower status of existence, which in religious terms was deemed a condition of sin. The mind represented the sought-for higher status of consciousness closer to the divine. Sexuality was a physical/body function, a base appetite totally unrelated to the mind and actually sought to dominate the mind and drag the human into an abyss of insatiable base yearnings or appetites. Once again the mission environment was seen as the place where the young Africans could be removed from their contaminated environment and schooled for elevated thought. Here they would be exorcised of all the sexual demons.

Among the Shona the mission church would still find elements they needed to confirm their myth of African sexuality. Here they found yet another African community at peace with its sexuality. Except for a thorough sex education from childhood to puberty, the Shona, who practiced neither male nor female circumcision, had no formally organized schools of puberty initiation rites.[7] As seen in chapter 1, through an elaborate Mutupo worldview, both boys and girls were raised to be open and comfortable with every aspect of human sexuality. It was also from within this worldview that the Shona youth learned that sex was never a casual matter. In the traditional setting, sexuality was affirmed and celebrated.[8] Shona art, poetry, oral literature, music, and dance were sensual, expressive of the joys of sexuality.

Early missionary women also approached the issues of sexuality with a degree of paranoia. At the mission young girls would be exorcised of African sexual demons by being socialized to adopt Victorian attitudes toward sexuality. Lawyer explains some of the mission strategies toward achieving this goal:

> We have learnt it is absolutely imperative that we lock our girls in at night. There is a reason. They would go out into the darkness, wander about and meet the school boys, or other boys; perhaps intruders would come into their huts. When Voondoo slept in my kitchen, I always attended to the locking up myself, the last thing before retiring. …To be sure one cannot keep the girls tied to one's apron string every minute of the day and night. They must go to the river to bathe, and they must make occasional visits to their people in the kraals. We have tried to teach them chastity, and the proper conduct of a Christian woman. But in spite of all our padlocks and keys, in spite of all our teaching, we have a little black baby on our hands. And I mean literally on our hands, for it is motherless and fatherless.[9]

At the mission, girls literally became prisoners by virtue of their gender. All the freedoms enjoyed in the old world vanished into thin air upon arrival at the mission. Here their movements inside and outside the mission center were confined to space granted by those in authority. They were monitored, chaperoned, or escorted at all times. Sexuality was not a topic for discussion on the mission campus. Yet ironically the whole world of the young girls was structured and organized around their sexuality vis-à-vis that of the boys. The subject would only be addressed in sermons. In this context sexuality was depicted as a lustful appetite that drove individuals into sin. The sexual urge needed to be tamed and suppressed at every level of the human experience if one were to attain true holiness.

At the boarding school young African girls would be psychologically circumcised through religious training. Sexual expression of any form was strictly prohibited. A religious worldview that totally denied human sexuality was promoted as the norm. In this environment the project began of grooming young Manyika girls into Victorian ladies as a necessary part of Christianization. Within a brief time of receiving training at Old Mutare, Mrs. Rasmussen felt confident that her students were becoming ladies. She portrays the the typical lady in these words:

> But she is very discreet in her conduct before these young men. When the young men are around she is the soul of demureness and often appears quite unaware that there is such a thing as a boy in the whole universe, let alone in her vicinity. . . . Nevertheless, when she gets on her best Sunday-go-to-meeting clothes, I fear her mind is not always on the sermon, as ours used to be, you know. A sly little Puss is "Sweet Sixteen" whether she be black or white.[10]

In matters of sexuality girls were socialized to be "demure" and view themselves as "sly" and "little" over against the overwhelming and possibly overpowering temptation of boys' sexuality. During these early years mission girls would be raised in a "sex-free" environment to preserve their chastity. Female virginity was a fixation of the mission church. Young women were expected to be "pure" on the day of their marriage. Male virginity was never in question in the mission church's vocabulary. By contrast, Manyika sexual norms and expectations were standard and applied to both sexes.

Influences such as the European-style pop music of the colonial culture eventually blew this bubble. Movies and pop music would not be liberating elements to mission girls. Instead they affirmed mission myths about women's sexuality. These influences depicted women as weak, passive, helpless, and emotional creatures who needed to be rescued from their misery by a strong male character. In this movie, music, and pop culture, girls were supposed to be beautiful and loving but insecure. Boys were to be aggressive, strong thinkers who lived to provide all that their women wanted. Women were supposed to want not sex or emotional support but material security. The man, on the other hand, was to want sex and the comfort of a faithful woman who stayed at home, waited on him, and took care of his every need.

Wives and Mothers

Early women at the mission inherited the leadership skills and pioneering spirit of their mentors; that is, early women missionaries. For example, having failed to secure native girls for school, Mrs. Rasmussen took over the running of the entire mission at Old Mutare. This meant that she was in charge of the school, farm, dormitory, and many other areas. She assumed all these duties on top of the translation work that she had been doing. Patterning themselves after their mentors, Manyika women as early evangelists' wives would wield considerable power in the new community. At the mission the new converts, as *Makhorwa* ("the saved ones"), would be groomed to constitute the nucleus of a new society. Upon marriage to each other they were expected either to stay on the mission lands or to be assigned to out-stations, where they were to evangelize and found new Christian communities.

As Makhorwa, the new converts were open to new cultural ideas and instruction, since they were expected to have renounced the pagan past. They were to become matriarchs and patriarchs to the new communities. They were allowed to draw wisdom and instruction only from two sources. First, they were to treat the Bible as a primary source from which to discern the ways of living a Christian life. Second, they were to draw on the ways of Western culture as lived out by their mentors.

The problem was that Western culture, as lived out by both missionaries and colonialists, claimed to be Christian and superior to indigenous culture. In this colonial context the lines of distinction between the Western culture of the church and that of the colony were always blurred. Individuals like Bishop Knight Bruce constantly struggled with this problem of how to draw the line between Christian and colonist-settler culture for the sake of the new African converts. He argued that the church ought to find ways of insulating the natives in general from what he called "European cultural vices," such as greed, deception, drink, cruelty, promiscuity, and cursing, which he claimed were so much part of the settler-colonialist ways.[11]

Gender

It was on the issues of gender that these early women converts began to struggle with an attempt to reconcile the two worlds apart from indigenous culture. The overlapping of missionary, Western Christianity, and Western colonial culture would become quite problematic in the area of gender relations. On the one hand, according to Methodism, the Bible pronounced women and men equal before God. As evangelists' wives, Manyika women would take the cue from the early missionary women and preach the gospel as well as perform most ministerial duties alongside their husbands. On the other hand, in the unfolding Western colonial culture men were said to be made of sterner stuff; and it was they who had permission to rule supreme. On the issue of gender the colonial world strictly held on to the dual-sphere ideology. Men were to be the leaders and actors in the public sphere and women were to belong to the private or domestic sphere. Even tough women who were alongside the men on the colonial front were never recognized or remembered as soon as the community was settled. In colonial southern Africa white women were gradually settled into the domestic sphere, where they were showered with gifts and teams of servants.

The early missionary church reconciled this gender conflict by espousing that women were equal but subordinate. According to Patricia Hill, a majority of the early missionary women, as products of the women's missionary society movements, were not seeking a revolution on issues of gender in or outside the church. They were not seeking equality with men. Rather, most of these women were at peace with themselves by accepting the equal but subordinate role in relationship to their men in church and society. Hill argues that nineteenth-century U.S.-American women in the women's missionary societies were generally seeking to expand their influence beyond the confines of the domestic sphere.[12]

Even though they were never recognized officially, missionary women expressed contentment with the "equal but subordinate" role to their missionary husbands. As mentioned before, this model of the early missionary woman as wife, mother, and teacher can be termed the "Mary Moffatt" model. Following this pattern, the model of a Christian's and pastor's wife was inculcated in the women in the new community of believers among the Manyika. A requirement in the curriculum for the theological training of pastors/evangelists was a study and an examination of the life of Mary Moffatt.[13]

Cecil Northcort gives a precise description of Mary Moffatt's relationship to her husband. For the fifty-three years they were married, he explains, she referred to her husband as "Moffatt." He continues:

> But there was a tender simplicity about their married life with Mary dutiful and Robert acceptably domineering in the Victorian domestic manner. It was all solid and sensible even though lived "amongst the blacks" beyond the range of organized civilities, for the Moffatts' home on the frontier was Mary's creation. If she was a little too clinging, and rather over fearful about her husband, it was all in the pattern of their married bliss and Moffatt liked it.[14]

As partners in ministry and wives to their husbands early missionary women went about their work contentedly. Zelma Lawyer conveys this sense of personal feelings of fulfillment and accomplishment as a woman in the role of mother, wife, and missionary, after receiving verses of poetry from her husband on her birthday:

> If anyone should suppose my life as a cook-trainer, a baby-bather, a soap-maker, a teacher of black women, to be a drab one, let him at once be assured that this is the happiest life I could imagine. I would not give it up for all the fine clothes, summer vacations, theatrical entertainments, and dinner parties that could be packed into any woman's existence. I do not want a hurried nerve-wracking life. This one is busy enough for me, and entertaining enough, and satisfying enough. I thank God for it every day I live. I sometimes imagine that it is all a dream from which I fear I may awaken, and find myself back in America. Though I know it is a blessed reality.[15]

In the latter part of this excerpt one can recognize the shift of focus toward the domestic role on the part of the early missionary wife. This shift toward domesticity was a gradual phenomenon in the colonial territories as they mirrored a similar trend in the West.[16] Like settler/colonial women, missionary women viewed themselves primarily as middle-class wives to their husbands and mothers to their children. Missionary women as wives retreated to the domestic sphere and even limited their involvement and participation in church affairs. In this role they were obsessed with the hiring, training, and firing of various household servants.[17]

As wives, it was not uncommon for a women to herald and praise her husband's accomplishments at her own expense. Women in the colonial context portrayed their men as naturally endowed with a superior intelligence necessary for leadership in both private and public spheres. For example, Zelma Lawyer uses words like *inventive, language shark, sober-minded, placid*, and *dutiful* to portray her husband George"s "character" and "intelligence." On this subject, Lawyer gives an interesting incident that occurred between her and her husband after an exceptional presentation showing his newly learned grasp of the Tonga language:

> After we had returned home, I said to Mrs. Rolls in George's presence, "I'll venture he's puffed up, all right, but just too modest to show it. I believe I'll puncture him with a pin and see if he will deflate." . . . And I really believe he thought for a split second that he had been deflated, when I popped a little candy sack in the vicinity of his left ear. I thought I had been rather clever, and said, "See? That's what happened when I stuck the pin in you."
>
> But he got ahead of me by saying he thought people ought to be able to control their feelings. When I saw that he thought I had been silly, I said, "I was only joking. You might know I had to have a little fun. I'm just proud of your accomplishments as I can be. Nobody else could have done it."
>
> "That's all right," he said. And he spoke no further about the evening's program. He seemed despondent. I wondered if he was working too hard, too long hours. Or was the climate getting him? To me the climate seemed perfectly grand. I can hardly understand why it affects the white man's health as it does. Perhaps I'll understand some day.[18]

Women and natives on the other hand were generally portrayed as lacking in these capabilities. Women were portrayed as emotional and fickle-minded. And native character was usually caricatured in physical terms. For example, in that same incident, Lawyer describes George's students' reaction to his performance this way: "[T]heir white eyes bulging out, their big hands went over their mouths, and still they grinned so broad that the grins extended beyond the boundaries of their hands." At Old Mutare Mrs. Rasmussen also gives a similar description of the character of one of her students at the mission, Jim Jijita:

> Jim's eyes fairly bulged with astonishment as he gazed at the marvelous array of finery while he rattled off a stream of ejaculations and favorable comments which would have led any hearer to think that there was the worst kind of row going on. I used to step to the door frequently to see if there was a fight in the kitchen until I got used to Jim's way of talking. Brow's bulldog at Broken Hill used to growl most viciously at me every time I saw him and first filled me with terror for he was a most savage looking brute. "Don't be afraid of him, that's his only way of talking," his master said. So it was: he'd trot along with me down the house growling all the way. He was perfectly harmless and good-natured. And so was Jim.[19]

In the colonial context such biases established as acceptable the social hierarchy, or pecking order, along the lines of race first and then gender. As early missionary women defined themselves more and more as mothers and wives, they left the public arena to their husbands and, together with settler women, endorsed a social structure in which the white male ruled supreme. In this social structure male, white aggressiveness was encouraged and tolerated as natural. Being black or female required submission and passivity. With this status assigned to them, white men in particular were invested with the ultimate power to control their women, the environment, and black women and black men. Any means necessary to coerce obedience or law and order were acceptable in the territories. As early as 1910, the Methodist Episcopal Church acknowledged in its resolutions that "grievous wrongs had been done to the native peoples." Whipping was the Conference's primary concern. The Conference exacted new laws forbidding the whipping of natives by any of its members.[20]

Wives

As wives to native evangelists, Manyika women were taught, first, the technical skills necessary for the operation of a Christian home and, second, the philosophical skills of wifehood and motherhood in this context. The women also learned these skills by observing the lives and listening to the stories of their teachers and mentors. As wives and mothers, African women would learn that, in the new worldview, they lived almost for the sole purpose of tending to the health and welfare of their husbands and children.

In the Christian community women were secondary to their husbands both inside and outside the home. Christian marriage, in conjunction with the colonial civil law, declared that an African woman remained a minor upon marriage. These women were nurtured to respect and defer authority on most matters to their husbands. The role of husband and father took on a new meaning for them. It was being elevated to a level at which men appeared to be the arbiters determining the lives of women in the church just as they did in the colonial world.

In church only men could be clergy and bishops, and in colonial society only men could be employed. Even those women who would later receive professional training as teachers and nurses at the mission would be forced to quit their careers when they got married.

Upon a Christian marriage women lost their family names and from then on would be addressed as "Mrs. So and So" or "Mother of So and So." Their ties to their community were severed since they were required to disassociate with a "primitive" past. Such severing of ties to the traditional extended family left women vulnerable to abuse. The woman would co-create a nuclear family in which the husband was designated as the head in all matters of survival and existence.

Coming from the West as it was, colonial Christianity was not the champion of women's rights, as it has historically claimed during this period. When the church, in conjunction with the colonial civil law, declared that upon Christian or civil marriage an African woman remained a minor, it meant women could not make contracts in business, own property, sue, claim custody of children, or initiate a divorce. Under the colonially created "Customary Law," African women were regarded literally as chattel to their husbands. For example, under these laws, the "father" assumed automatic custody of any child born outside of marriage; and his custody could not be contested in any court of law. In such a case, if the couple involved were young and the young man had "no interest" in marriage, he was required by law to pay a compensatory "damage" to the young woman's father if it were known that she was a virgin upon the first encounter. The term *damage* shows that in colonial law women were property. They belonged to their father at birth and then to their husbands upon marriage.

In the colonial world a Christian marriage was not the liberating Magna Charta that the early missionary church professed it was for the African woman but rather a document that reversed almost all the human rights women had enjoyed in the indigenous community. With this document African women would lose not only their rights to self-determination in the public arena but also their sexual and reproductive rights. Matters of fertility, sexuality, contraception, and reproduction would no longer be a woman's affair but a public affair for policy formulation by the leadership of the church and the colonial state. This area of women's health would be fundamentally neglected in both the government and the mission hospitals. For example, even Shearly Cripps would found a "men's only" venereal diseases clinic at Maronda Mashanu. Obviously, women were victimized as they contracted these colonial diseases from their husbands, who were coming home from the mines and cities in South Africa. Dr. Samuel Gurney (Conference medical director, physician at Nyadiri mission hospital, 1923) reports that these sexually transmitted diseases were imported into the region:

> The presence of these diseases among the native people is comparatively a recent innovation. When I came to this country twenty years ago and for several years after that time I never saw a single case, but when the infection was finally introduced, it spread like wild fire until now the whole country is full of it. There are whole villages that are gradually being destroyed by reason of these diseases. Some time ago

a company of young men came to me from one of the stations where we have mission-work and begged me to come and save men from the destruction that was going on by reason of these diseases.[21]

Despite these restrictions, it is important to underscore that the first African Christian women converts, as wives of evangelists, were a powerful group. During this formative stage of the church they, without hesitation, inherited their mentors' power and influence in the new community. It was with this spirit of pioneering that they founded the Rukwadzano movement organization. In their role as Bible women they preached and ministered in their new communities. Their names and work were even recognized in the Conference minutes. For example, the following six names of Bible women appear in the 1909 Conference minutes of the Methodist Episcopal Church: Mufambiswa Caplen, Fumandiswa Chimbadzwa, Mutiziswa Peranyi, Mukonyerwa Mari, Mary Matimba, Matingapasi Sakutombo. Together with their evangelist husbands, these women recognized themselves as the architects of a new society. Their role in this new community was that of *Mai*, or "Mother," of the community. They felt competently trained for the role. While their husbands were receiving industrial training, they were also receiving training for operating a Christian home. As Bible women they, like their men, had learned to read and write. With the power of literacy they not only acquired the ability to read the scriptures of the new religion by themselves but were also positioned to instruct others on the subject.

But as time went on, their new role as Mai of the community would shrink in power and influence as they were being pushed into the confines of the domestic sphere. The colonial culture in and outside the church was silently forcing them into a culture of domesticity. This role of colonial motherhood and wifehood often called them to submission and sacrifice. On the other hand, the role of *Baba* (Father) was accruing power and authority. New landmarks clearly stipulating a subordinate status of wives in relation to their husbands were appearing. According to Mbuya Masevha (pioneer member but not one of the founders), "Before colonial Christianity the word *Baba* in Shona meant only one's father. It was

Rukwadzano/Christianity that taught us that a woman addresses her husband as *Baba*. Before Christianity, women would address or call their husbands by their first name, such as "Mhondiwa, come here!"[22]

Mothers

African Christian women were instructed on how they could best fill their role as mothers. The instructions were primarily in two areas. First they were introduced to the technical aspects of raising a new generation of the new community. Here women were taught skills of hygiene, appropriate clothing for children, and the proper manners and etiquette of child-rearing. Second, the women were taught a new understanding of the role of Christian motherhood. In this area they learned that the life of a mother was to be one of long-suffering, self-denial, and self-sacrifice in order to set an example and to guide her children's path toward salvation. In the Rukwadzano movement they founded, a mother would be blamed and disciplined by the group if her daughter got pregnant outside of marriage. Nothing happened to her if her son got a girl pregnant.

Early missionary women were quick to the rescue of young women who became mothers at the mission on matters of how to raise the new generation of Christians. They were repulsed by the way African babies were raised and generally felt that there was nothing to learn from the traditional methods of mothercraft. African children in infancy were depicted either as little rascals smothered as a result of too much adult and sibling attention or as a filthy, naked lot suffering severe neglect.

The expectation for native Christian women was to learn new mothering skills. The church would also introduce them to a new lifestyle in which they acquired new tastes. This new lifestyle replicated the Western colonial lifestyle in almost every detail. As mothers, women were introduced to new foods or diets, new styles of dress, and new house utensils and furnishings that were considered mandatory for a Christian home. In this capacity Christian women and men developed into the biggest consumer class for colonial goods. For example, as early as 1905 the Christian lifestyle for a young couple at Old Mutare began with a wedding ceremony for which both the bride and the groom had to buy appropriate wedding attire.

Mrs. Rasmussen expresses her dilemma on the mission's role in creating consumers for the colonial economy as she gives an account of Kaduku's experiences when buying a trousseau for his wedding in Mutare:

> There are two kind of stores to be found in all European towns in Africa, the so-called Kaffir Store where only natives and Indians trade and the White Stores where Europeans deal and where large profits are also gathered from native trade. Many white men will curse the Kaffir roundly and the mission which pampers him so that he gets above his place. But if he comes into the same man's store with a handful of yellow sovereigns in his pocket, why, that's only business. This same man will spend a whole morning waiting on such a native, taking down everything he has on his shelves and showing him, for the time being, all the deference that he would to the mayor or president of the local bank. Kaduku knew a man who kept one of the best stores for whites and straight to him he went.[23]

In Christian motherhood Manyika women also came to learn that they were expected to live lives of devoted piety and self-sacrifice for the sake of their children. As the culture of domesticity tightened its grip on Manyika women in this new world, they were nurtured and encouraged to believe that they existed only for the giving of themselves to their children and husbands. They were expected to live lives of exemplary piety and cleanliness in order for their children to emulate them. In this role, women were cast as morally superior to men by nature. Women's moral superiority was said to have stemmed from an intrinsic element in their being that caused them to be exceptionally receptive and responsive to the message and principles of religion.

In the nineteenth-century Protestant Christian worldview religion was understood as a matter primarily of the heart or emotions. Women were also understood as overwhelmingly emotional beings. By this token women were deemed the custodians of morals and men the custodians of reason. In this context, women as mothers were assigned the task of nurturing children to become well-integrated individuals as adults. Mothers were to assume total responsibility for the physical, emotional, moral, and intellectual development of each child in their home. The prescription for the successful achievement of such a task was for women to live lives of piety and purity. In her essay "Women and Revivalism," Martha Tomhave Blauvelt cites Reverend Ashbel Green's conservative view on defining the boundaries for women and their roles in religion in nineteenth-century U.S. America. One of the tasks he defined as proper for women is the raising of children, which he explained as follows:

> Secondly, it is one of the peculiar and most important duties of Christian women, to instruct, and pray with children, and to endeavor to form their tender minds to piety, intelligence, and virtue. Here is a wide fertile field of their appropriate labors, in the service and honor of their Redeemer. The earliest years of children are usually and necessarily past, almost wholly, under female care, and it is much earlier than is commonly supposed, that their minds and moral feelings take cast, which is often as lasting as life. Of what inconceivable importance it is then, that this first molding of the mind and heart should be favorably made; and that mothers should know and remember that if so made, it must commonly be made by them. They have the capacity of mingling, as it were, their own souls with the souls of their children— of breathing into them, with a maternal tenderness and sympathy for which there can be no substitute, those sentiments of filial reverence for their Creator and Redeemer, and of veneration for all that is holy and lovely in the religion of the Gospel, which, under the Divine blessing, may become, and do often in fact become, the germs of early and vital godliness.[24]

Early Christian Manyika women received most of this nineteenth-century understanding on the role of motherhood from the missionaries. In this role women directly assumed the responsibility and accountability for their children's success or failure in life. By contrast, for the Mutupo principle the success or failure of a child is a shared communal responsibility and accountability. In this context children are raised by a community that constantly admonishes them by all means to avoid any ways that will provoke a mother's wrath or anger.[25] A mother's sacrifices at pregnancy and birth were perceived as all sufficient, and a child or community had no right to demand any more of her. In the Shona context women as mothers were to be shown adoration by alleviating any causes of their pain, suffering, or discomfort. Mothers owed the community nothing; but the community owed mothers everything, from the health and happiness of their children to that of their environment, their husbands, and themselves.

Motherhood in missionary Christianity was defined in perfectionist terms as solely a woman's duty. When successful, women were to be humble, not claiming credit or compensation; but when they failed, were to be accountable and hold themselves to blame. A daughter's pregnancy outside of marriage was often regarded as a mother's fault.[26] Among the Manyika, Christian motherhood socialized women to focus their lives on the caring and raising of children. This focus on children would intensify in the colonial culture of domesticity, in which black mothers and children were pushed to the edges of existence in the "Reserves," where they were treated as marginal and dispensable.

Women who came to the mission and trained as professional women in limited areas, such as nursing and teaching, were generally thought to be seeking to expand the domestic sphere. Within a colonial economy that was crushing all forms of African initiatives toward survival or self-determination, women's jobs were regarded as a privilege and not a right, thus providing no job security. They became real beasts of burden, struggling to balance professional careers and colonial-church expectations of the roles of motherhood and wifehood.

The early mission work among Manyika women by U.S.-American women missionaries at Old Mutare failed to liberate, as intended, because of two factors. First, the curriculum designed for the women's education was based on a colonial myth postulating that all the young women who came to the mission were cultural refugees fleeing an oppressive society. Women missionaries therefore designed an education that sought to reject Manyika culture totally and to superimpose European culture, a culture they regarded as superior and compatible with the Christian religion. Through mission boarding-school education Victorian images of womanhood were adopted and taught as the ideal.

Second, women missionaries at Old Mutare also failed to acknowledge that colonization and colonialism were the root cause of pain and suffering among Manyika women. In its quest for mission sites, guaranteed security, and permanent settlement, the church compromised its prophetic voice. Instead, the church was coerced to participate in or endorse colonial government schemes designed to destroy all expressions of resistance and exploit or curtail every aspect of Manyika women's search for self-determination. As colonialism entrenched itself deeper into the economic and social fabric, the Shona and Ndebele mission education contributed very little toward equipping women for liberation.

The education curriculum designed by early missionary women for the first Manyika women at Old Mutare heavily emphasized religion. Along with education in the domestic arts, missionary women taught the fundamentals of the new religion. The early women graduates were educated to be religious educators themselves. In this process the women were introduced to the worldview of the Bible. With everything falling apart around them, some of them embraced the message of the new religion and sought to appropriate it in their own context.

CHAPTER 5

The Birth of Rukwadzano

THERE ARE TWO VERSIONS, BOTH OFFICIAL, OF THE DATE AND HISTORY OF THE beginning of Rukwadzano. The first version is that of the mission church, found in the 1928 minutes of the Rhodesia Mission Conference of the Methodist Episcopal Church, as well as in the first edition of the women's organization's official Handbook and Constitution, *Rumano Rwe Rukwadzano* (1938).[1] The second version, the Manyika version, is found in the 1944 edition of *Rumano* (revised again 1960, corrected 1974). Both editions agree that the organization was initiated through the Women's Conference in 1929. Beyond that, the two versions agree little about who founded the organization and why.

According to the church version, Rukwadzano began at the initiative of the mission church to organize women for instruction in the duties and obligations of "Christian motherhood." The second version, subtlely conveyed in the 1944 edition, notes that Lydia Chimonyo and other women founded Rukwadzano as a women's prayer group that met discreetly outside the mission-church grounds to call upon the power of the Holy Spirit to guide them as Christian women.

An analysis of the two versions reveals why historians have differed on the interpretation of this group of church women. Those who accept the church's version have tended to portray church women's organizations in southern Africa as mediums of systemic oppression designed by mission Christianity. Women in these groups are depicted as victims of both the "Christian culture of domesticity" and a vestigial traditional past. Such scholars generally associate these women with prayer and a cult of motherhood in which they wail penitentially for God to, for example, preserve their daughters' virginity.[2]

Those who take the Manyika version join the ranks of a few scholars who have begun to study these groups as representatives of an authentic African women's response and initiative to Christianity in a colonial context. These scholars consider women in these organizations to have demanded and secured a voice with which they called for transformation both inside and outside of the church.[3]

The Manyika Version

According to the 1944 edition of *Rumano*, Rukwadzano started as an initiative of Manyika women to form a seminary-campus women's prayer group. Lydia Chimonyo, a pastor/teacher's wife at Old Mutare who loved prayer and deeply believed in the power of the Holy Spirit to change situations, went around campus in search of other women with similar convictions. She found them, and they started a prayer group. Under her leadership, the group began by meeting for prayer in the woods just before carrying their firewood home. Later, the group decided to specify a time and a place for daily meetings. They picked 4:00 A.M. as the time for meeting at a site in the westerly direction. The group named their western site *paChingando* ("a place of deep contemplation and meditation"). Then they chose another site in the easterly direction and named it *paDara* ("the watchtower").

The corrected 1974 edition mentions that during this period Lydia Chimonyo was given a hard time about where and from whom she drew her authority to lead the prayer group. It is worth noting a textual difference between the Shona and the English translation of the seventh paragraph. In this paragraph the two translations mention two different groups as the "tormentors" of Lydia Chimonyo. The Shona version says they were *Vanhu* (people in general). The English version calls them "church leaders" who gave her a hard time and often asked her through whose wisdom she did her work.[4]

The text clearly states that Lydia Chimonyo was the founding mother of the prayer group that was later organized into Rukwadzano Rwe Wadzimai We Methodist. It also underscores that at its founding, the group and its leader were viewed with suspicion if not outright hostility. Finally, there is no woman missionary in the membership of the committee that put together the organization's handbook. The names of the committee are given as follows:

    Edith Marange, Chair
    Naomi Mandisodza, Secretary
    Martha Mudzengerere
    Lydia Mandizera
    Rezen Chieza
    Lydia Zimonte
    Lillian Machiri
    Esther Jangano

A critical study of some sections of the 1944 version about the founding, nature, and development of Rukwadzano will show that it was a Manyika Christian women's movement with a message and mission to build a sustainable community in the midst of the ravages of colonial oppression. The women were seeking to belong to a community that acknowledged the hurt and suffering inflicted by European colonialism and sought to bring an end to this source of evil. And finally they desired a community that was present to heal the hurt and suffering of an oppressed land and its people.

Further study of their praxis shows women who drew inspiration from an "unwritten text" that gave them courage to undermine whatever principle in the mission-church doctrine appeared to be an obstacle in their search for a redeemed and redeeming community here on earth.

Drawing from the Bible and the Shona worldview, these women reconstructed a message and mission that not only critiqued mission-church Christianity but also created new models for envisioning church and community. For example, Rukwadzano's understanding of salvation comes directly from the Manyika worldview in which the word *Rukwadzano* means "united for sustenance and survival."

The Conference Version

The official minutes of the 1928 Rhodesia Mission Conference present a second version on the beginning of Rukwadzano. According to this version Rukwadzano started as an initiative and recommendation of the Committee on the State of the Church. After coming up with the recommendation for a "native women's organization," the Committee proceeded to request the Women's Conference (which was comprised of all women missionaries) to submit a plan for the organization.[5] In 1938 the Committee recommended "the organization of the native women of our church to be called Rukwadzano We Methodist." This time a committee comprised of both Manyika and missionary women was formed and assigned the responsibility of framing a constitution for the organization. In this version, there is no mention anywhere that Rukwadzano began as a prayer group under Lydia Chimonyo. Indeed, Mrs. Chimonyo is listed merely as one of the members of the committee.

Mrs. Obadiah [Lydia] Chimonyo	*Reserve Members*
Mrs. Mayibaya	Mrs. J. Rugayo
Mrs. Samuel Chieza	Mrs. Phillip Chieza
Mrs. Job Tsiga	Mrs. Mature
Mrs. Titus Marange	Mrs. Josiah Ghimbadzwa
Mrs. Enoch Munjoma	Mrs. G. Roberts
Mrs. F. Quinton	Mrs. M. J. Murphree

These minutes and reports of the church portray Rukwadzano as an organization of women who had made a personal commitment through baptism and marriage to stay in their place as women and wives and to be good and faithful to the church and their husbands. Women were to stay at home and raise Christian children and at the end of their lives expect a reward in heaven.

The church's minutes report that Rukwadzano started on recommendation of the Women's Conference, composed of all missionary women or wives, and not as an initiative of Manyika women. Second, the structure and texts given in the 1938 edition of the *Rumano* Handbook and Constitution overwhelmingly reflect the organization as nothing more than a clone of mission-church orthodoxy in structure and doctrine.

The church's official version illustrates how this women's movement was being tamed into a church organization. In this case the church achieved this objective through the superimposition of a constitution and leadership of missionary wives and Manyika male clergy. The 1928 select committee for organizing a "native women's organization" consisted of six African women and three missionary wives. Advisors for the Northern region during this period are listed as the following: Reverend M. J. Murphree, Reverend J. Chimbadzwa, Reverend O. Chimonyo, and Reverend T. Marange. During this initial period, the church imposed its will through this committee. The committee constantly rejected and stifled any of the women's initiatives toward self-determination. The church was always aware that underneath this imposed veneer of mission-church orthodoxy lay a seething cauldron of oppressed women's cries for freedom. These cries were muffled further by colonial studies insisting that these women's groups were nothing but puppets dancing to the mission church's tunes.

Church Doctrine

In the primary interest of conserving tradition and doctrine, the Methodist Episcopal Church Conference commissioned the Women's Conference, comprised exclusively of missionary women, to organize the African women. When Bishop Hartzell recommended the founding of this Women's Conference in 1910, he suggested that it be an auxiliary to the Annual Conference with the special mission of seeking "to uplift women of this land."[6] Minutes of the Methodist Episcopal Church show that the Women's Conference focused on improving the lives of African women by grooming them into suitable wives for the pastors and teachers or suitable candidates for domestic service in the colonial households. The education of these women was grounded in religious and domestic training. Early women missionaries like Mrs. M. J. Murphree used the constitution to fashion the organization to reflect the objectives they had set to accomplish as a church. In this situation they were being called upon by the church to "tame" an African women's movement into an organization that would both reflect the church's doctrine and pursue its agenda for African women.

The fundamental doctrines of the church were reflected in the organization's methods for membership recruitment and the structure and form of the organization. Membership requirements reflected the church's evangelical understanding of sin and salvation. Also, the structure and rules of the organization revealed a legalistic and militaristic approach to governing the lives of the members; at every level of the structure there was a rigid hierarchy that mirrored the ecclesiastical structure of the mission church.

Membership requirements indicate a change between 1928 and 1944. The 1928 requirements were clear and specific. During this first phase, membership in the organization regarded evidence of personal salvation as a primary and necessary sign of one's renunciation of sin and of a "heathen past." By contrast, in 1944, all the requirements were compressed into the status of being a full member of the Methodist Church.[7] The select committee of 1928 came up with the following specific requirements for membership into the organization:

1. Clear testimony of present and personal salvation.
2. Fair knowledge of the catechism.
3. Refrain from night dancing.
4. Reasonable attendance and giving the support of the church.
5. Christian marriage if both are Christians.
6. The possession of the New Testament and Hymnal, if literate.[8]

A Mission Theology at Old Mutare

During this formative phase of Rukwadzano, membership was based on two qualifications. Prospective members would first have to be converted and then undergo a process of learning the organization's belief and doctrine. The 1914 minutes of *The Rhodesia Missionary Advocate* underscored this process and the relationship of evangelism, organization, and education:

> Evangelism brings a man to Christ but he must undergo a process of mental and spiritual education before he is admitted into membership of the Church. Evangelization and education are a span going on as one. They are Siamese twins. Evangelism must issue in organization and education and these in turn are evangelistic. We must not limit

evangelism to the conversion of the individual. We are to seek the conversion of tribes, provinces and nations. Organization and education make this possible over a long stretch of time.[9]

Consistent with its tradition the Methodist Church was gaining membership rapidly through the revival-meeting campaigns. It was in these campaigns that the Christian religion was introduced through preaching, and individuals were invited to become members. In the revivalist tradition, one converted after a rebirth experience by renouncing her or his sin, accepting Jesus as personal savior, and beginning a new life. After this experience an individual was initiated through baptism and nurtured into the Christian worldview through teaching. In the teachings of the Methodist mission, church women were taught a new worldview that rejected their cultural experience and granted them a limited role in the freedom to interpret the scriptures from their own perspective. They were nurtured into an expression of faith that was rigidly dualistic as well as hierarchical.

Conversion and Salvation

The Methodist mission church's understanding of conversion and salvation at Old Mutare could be characterized as having evolved within the contextual realities faced by the church in the region. Minutes of the first Conferences are replete with missionary testimonies on how and when they were "saved" before accepting the call to mission in the foreign field. Most of these conversions are traced back to either a camp or a revival meeting.

In these testimonies missionaries testified to the inward personal experience of being "saved" and related that such an experience was accompanied by a call to duty or mission. These missionaries clearly defined their mission in the foreign field as that of saving "heathens" from Islam, Catholicism, and Animism to "Evangelical" Christianity. The vision of the church in these foreign lands was to create communities that "lived by the Book," meaning primarily the New Testament. Missionaries set out to preach what they defined as a message of salvation from paganism and to practice works of mercy among peoples in the "foreign lands." They envisioned the birth of new communities in which the gospel would bring about democracy, love, peace, and harmony in place of what they perceived as the tyranny of archaic, primitive cultures. Their vision was to establish communities where there would be no more tears, weeping, or death.

At Old Mutare, as in most of colonial southern Africa, this vision of such a Christian community became an illusive dream. In the context of brutal colonial conquests and settlement by a people of their own race and homelands, the message and mission of these Methodists became blurred. From the start, the church realized it was in double jeopardy because it was aware that, even before colonial conquests, the native people had shown no interest in the Christian message. By the colonial period, they were facing a progressively hostile audience in a majority of the native peoples. Therefore, in search of personal security and institutional establishment the mission church briefly shared the same bed with the colonialists—and a symbiotic relationship was born. Thus the church compromised by blunting the edge of its message so as to gain favors with the new masters of the land.[10]

In the process the mission church adopted the masters' language and worldview. The latter's blueprint for the new society was drawn from the Old Testament as well as the burgeoning scientific European worldview of industrial capitalism. From the Old Testament colonial society created a myth that viewed European settlers as the chosen people of God and southern Africa as the land of promise to be possessed and settled by any means necessary.[11] Settling the land and subduing or massacring the native peoples was deemed a divine mandate. Informed by Darwinist evolutionary theory, this worldview was hierarchical at every level. Categories of race, color, class, nature, and gender were viewed in opposition, in competition, and in hierarchical order. An article entitled "The People of Rhodesia" in *The Rhodesia Mission Advocate* captures the Methodist mission-church's views on race:

> In Rhodesia there are three races; viz. the white, the black, and the brown or Indian. The latter are of the lower class, coolies, who carry on trade with the natives. The white race is principally English, though

the Dutch and Scotch are here in increasing numbers. There are but a very few Americans. The Irish give a humorous sprinkling, while the indomitable Jew has his share in business. The black man is civil. In passing he bares his head and gives the entire path. He treats the white man as superior.[12]

After accepting the colonial worldview as sensible and legitimate, the church redefined its message and mission to suit the context and situation. At Old Mutare the church revised its message, mission, and understanding of conversion and salvation. In a compromise with colonial settlers and colonialism the mission church suddenly saw itself preaching the gospel of spreading what it called a "Christian civilization." The writings of the period reveal that the church's mission among the first pupils at the mission was to wean them from their traditional communities, give them industrial or ministerial training, and immerse them into the new "Christian, colonial industrial culture." The religious training received by the first group of converts became a complex concoction of selective New Testament theology mixed with the colonial views of society and the universe.

In this environment, the words *sin*, *redemption*, *conversion*, and *salvation* were relativized or subjected to selective interpretation by the missionaries. For example, apart from sin meaning "wrongful acts" or the original condition at birth as held by Methodist beliefs, for converts sin also came to be associated with being black, African, female, or poor. In its struggle to implant itself among the people, the mission church quickly adopted the colonial approach of conquest and exploitation through force by demonizing every element of the native peoples.

Color

The early mission church almost literally saw the world in black-and-white terms. Categories, characteristics, and conditions were created to fit individuals and groups by the color of their skin. The colors of the two peoples, African and European, came to symbolize bipolar realities in which one was terminally right or wrong, good or evil, superior of inferior. For example, there was no word for "sin as an act" in Manyika worldview. The word *black* as a color assumed a new meaning in the mission church. It was translated in the Methodist theological terminology as "sin" or an "act of sin" (*chitema*), or generally became a symbol of all that is evil. *Black* denoted the Africans and their culture, all of which was perceived as impure, ugly, filthy, guilty, and undesirable. All of this is alien to Manyika/Shona culture. In this culture, *black* and *white* were complementary dimensions symbolic of the color spectrum. They were the colors of the ancestors. Both were regarded as sacred colors by the Hungwe people.[13]

Christianity also introduced the concept of Satan or the Devil in anthropomorphic terms. In pictorial as well as conceptual imagery this figure was portrayed by the color black or resembled all the characteristics associated with the Africans. This was quite consistent with a long Christian tradition that had sought to personify or objectify evil and perceive it as an active force. The anthropomorphizing of evil into Satan or the Devil moved the location of evil from the individuals within a community to a force or being outside the community. Further, this being or force was portrayed as different in nature or appearance from anything or anyone in the white community or tradition.

The problem is that the personification of evil creates a "face" that does not resemble the community. In Western Christianity the Devil's face has been either that of women or of a non-European race, particularly "blacks." This imagery left an indelible mark on the psyche of colonized and Christianized black peoples. First, they were barraged with messages and imagery that indicted them as the personification of evil and all that was irredeemable in human nature. They were taught self-hate. Second, instead of locating and naming the source of their pain and suffering, colonized and Christianized people turned inward in search of the Devil. As victims of a genocidal system, they resorted to self-blame.

This syndrome of self-hate and self-blame still persists even in post-independence Africa. Social critics have attempted to address the issue through music, art, and other forms of expression. For example, the 1991 album *Corruption* by musician Thomas Mapfumo contains a piece entitled *"Handina Munyama Iwe Shamwari"* ("I am not cursed, my friend"). In this piece, Mapfumo rejects the view of Africans as a cursed people. Such a misinformed view of the sources of evil needlessly saps a people's energy and causes them tremendous pain, suffering, and death.[14] Evil social systems are able to use this tactic to buy time for self-entrenchment and flourishing, while inflicting as much pain as possible on their victims.

The color *white* came to represent the opposite of "blackness." Associated with the color of European people and their civilization and lifestyle, in the church *white* came to symbolize innocence, good news, cleanliness, beauty, purity, and the desirable. Hymns in the Methodist Hymnal (*Ngoma*) that highlighted this "color syndrome" were not uncommon. With English subtitles such as "Whiter than Snow," lyrics were charged with racial overtones. For example, hymn 138 repeatedly fed into the chorus lines that read, *"Ndinofarira, sukai ndichene, Ndichene, ndichene kudai semwimwi"* ("Please wash/cleanse me until I am clean/white, Until I am as white/clean, as white/ clean as you"). The "you" in this case is Jesus or God. It mattered to the mission church that Jesus was "white."

The imagery of lightness and darkness was overly dramatized in mission theology. Day and night were objectified to signify whiteness as lightness of race and blackness as darkness of race. Daylight came to be the time when "innocent" people transacted and did business and prospered. Any business or act done during the day was fair and free. Nighttime was when "evil" people acted, plotted, did their business, danced and did immoral things (e.g., having sex). The church banned all nighttime activities for its converts. Night was when most Shona communities had fun together or sat to discuss family affairs. Heaven, or paradise, was often portrayed as a place of light. Here, there was no night but eternal day; and God's glory beamed and shone so brightly it blinded all around "Him."

The church also introduced wearing black as the symbol of death and mourning. Widowed women were required to wear black at all times during the mourning period, which often lasted a lifetime because the church strictly discouraged remarriage of widowed women (but not of widowed men). The Christian colonial construct of color created a cosmology in which the devil and all that was evil were personified in the color of Africans. The Savior, or Christ, figure and all that was good and moral were personified in the color of Europeans.[15]

On Women

On gender, the mission church picked up on the colonial pioneer culture that glorified and credited white men as brave achievers, creators, and innovators of civilization. They were also cast as agents of progress and prosperity, as well as custodians of truth as law and order. White women were portrayed at best as paragons of beauty and "chastity," but this beauty was cast as a source of male corruption or evil. Wise men were advised by all means to shun the influence of a woman or to "master" the art of deceitful flattery when dealing with women. Women were regarded as weak in all matters of self-determination, flawed and irrevocably inferior to men.

From the Bible and Western tradition the mission church generally scapegoated women as the source of evil. The Genesis 3 narrative as a myth of creation came to dictate how women were regarded in this new culture and religion. In this narrative the woman is specifically implicated with the serpent as a co-agent or vehicle of evil in the community. Thus her very nature is viewed as the embodiment of evil. In church or culture a woman becomes a force to conquer, destroy, or silence. The mission church gradually chose to silence its women and supported any colonial schemes that sought to put African women in their place.

Such allegations have been supported by budding Zimbabwean "feminist" scholars, such as Dangarebgwa and Gaidzanwa. Rudo Gaidzanwa has shown that, until 1980, Shona/Ndebele fictional publications that were promoted and used as high-school literature texts by the Rhodesia Literature Bureau were overwhelmingly written by men, particularly Christian or mission-educated men. A common theme in this literature is the depiction of women as villains in men's lives and thus by this very nature and character deserving of affliction or cruel deaths. Women characters—mothers, daughters, aunts, lovers, or wives—are depicted as deceitful liars, witches, or prostitutes whose lives are spent seeking and plotting to torment the men inside and outside their lives. The punishment for these women—torture, rape, dismemberment, destitution, and lonely old age—is deemed justified. Gaidzanwa's writing successfully illustrates that this Christian theology of associating women with evil permeated not only the Christian but also the non-Christian literate Zimbabwean community.[16]

An example of the continued, pervasive influence of this theology on the psyche and popular culture of Zimbabwe is evidenced by Matawire's 1988 popular musical album, which won a prestigious "Presidential Award" despite the fact that the number one and most promoted piece on the album perpetuated the myth of the connection of women and evil. Matawire's piece *Diaboro Nyoka?* is an outstanding musical composition, but its lyrics are drawn from the Genesis 3 narrative on the origin of evil. Even in its own artistic and "innocent" way, the piece perpetuates the Christian myth of indicting women as the sources or embodiments of evil.

On the Poor

When it came to the issues of the poor, the mission church spoke out of both sides of its mouth. On one side, the church quietly supported conquest and settlement schemes designed to totally dispossess Africans of their dignity and from access to the means of survival. Such a process turned the colonial and missionary mythical image of the totally depraved African into a reality for the Manyika. The church placed the cause of the abject poverty of the Manyika in their perceived laziness, ignorance, and mediocrity.

On the other side, the church claimed that those who converted to Christianity were the chosen few who prospered materially along with white people because of their favored standing with God. Material prosperity signaled a condition of "being blessed" by the deity because one not only was saved but also was living according to God's laws. Those materially poor were cast as unbelievers and sinners who constantly violated God's law. But for the African Christians the church also had a contradictory message on this gospel of wealth. It cautioned them that "the love of money was the root of all evil" and therefore strongly warned them against the love of the material things of this world.

In the context of brutal and fine-tuned colonial schemes of dispossession the church alleged that the impoverished state of the Manyika was a self-inflicted wound stemming from a stagnant culture and civilization. With this rationale, the church unapologetically treated the African poor as fair game for derision and contempt. In this formative phase, the church was not nurtured to notice or listen to the stories or the voices of the poor. With silent arrogance the church refused to define poverty and its root causes in their true context. Instead of fighting government policies and schemes, it advanced the colonial cause by offering irrelevant solutions that also were meant to serve its own interests. For example, individuals representing the church, like Mr. Alvord, missionary of the American Board, rose to the highest rank of government public service while claiming that African rural poverty was a result not of the poor lands allocated to them but of the ancient methods of farming the people still used. Claiming to have experimented and produced miraculous results with students at the mission, Alvord joined the government in order to take his revolution to Africans in the whole territory.[17]

A Manyika idiom goes *Urombo Uroyi* ("Poverty is an evil spell"). Two ideas are communicated here. First, poverty is a state of emergency. If ignored, it is a poison that will literally kill an individual or community. Second, poor individuals or a poor community should not rest until they have identified the source or cause of their suffering and pain. At this point the church neither saw the poverty of the Manyika as an emergency nor did it genuinely seek its causes. With such beginnings the church over the years would train and nurture individuals who never took issues of the poor seriously. As the new elites, mission-church graduates often severed roots with their rural poor kinfolk or viewed them with contempt and conde-scension. In another way they were viewed as relics of a distant past who resisted change and reaped the bitter fruits of such folly. The new elites felt they made the right decisions and choices and had the right to enjoy fruits of their virtue unperturbed.

For those who converted to Christianity, the church preached a contradictory gospel of guaranteed material prosperity for people living a "Christian lifestyle" and a gospel of admonishment to those members who invested all their energies in pursuit of "treasures of this world." The first part of this message of guaranteed Christian prosperity was believable in the early phase of the church's mission, because it was only its converts who received training at its centers and could be hired as skilled laborers in the colonial industrial economy. Those who chose farming were guaranteed success because, while non-Christians were being repatriated into the desert or "reserves," they could stay and access the fertile mission lands owned by the church. Mission Christians were cast as the chosen ones, as evidenced by their success and prosperity in terms of holding prestigious jobs and owning property such as furniture or plows in the new colonial system.

Though prosperous, however, Christians were often admonished to obey all authority and accept their social standing related to that of white people. For example, in the 1930 Conference Minutes, the Committee on the State of the Church gives this recommendation: "Christians should set examples of loyalty to the government, giving special attention to obeying laws, such as that of paying taxes on time."[18] The mission church never preached a gospel of equality or justice on the issues of race and wealth. White wealth was portrayed as justly acquired by a racial group whose ingenuity was supposedly far superior to that of black people.

A second message that was very loud and clear in mission-church theology admonished Christians to refrain from the pursuit of wealth. On this subject the church emphasized its dualistic view of the universe: this world was regarded as materialist and evil as opposed to the spiritual world where people need neither bread nor butter to survive. Anyone in search of comfortable shelter, sufficient food, and funds was considered to seek too many fleshly comforts. A gospel of otherworldliness became an easy way out for the mission church as, by the 1930s, it began to realize that colonization and colonialism were strangling the breath out of a whole region.

Even the church and its missionaries were no longer at ease. For example, the Reverend C. Gates, District Superintendent of Mutare, expressed frustration and accused the State of what he termed a deplorable attitude toward missions and missionaries. Gates begins by pointing out that, despite the increased government grant from the new Department of Native Development, the situation was far from beneficial to the church's work. On the issue of government grants and mission schools, he notes:

> From the earliest of days Native churches and schools have gone hand in hand. We admit that grants ought to be conditioned upon recipient's acting reasonable and sticking to regulations. But grants can be gained at too high a price, and if independence, joy, and happiness in missionary work have to be sacrificed in order to get them, it would be better to discontinue to accept them. We are missionaries sent out to preach the Gospel, commissioned by our church "to make the Lord Jesus Christ known to all men as their Divine Savior."[19]

Under the rubric of perceiving reality dualistically—split between spirit and matter, heaven and earth—the mission church was able to delay confronting the state on issues of justice and human rights. It preached a gospel that called individuals to repent and be baptized in preparation for the day they would meet their Maker. At death, one faced either reward/heaven or eternal punishment/hell. The way to heaven was paved by renouncing the things of this world and walking the narrow path of obedience, forgiveness, and love even for one's enemies. Popular hymns like No. 211 in the Methodist Hymnal underscored this theology of renunciation:

Handichadi kuva nyope	I renounce laziness
Handichadi mari zhinji	I renounce lots of money
Handichadi pfuma huru	I renounce wealth
Ngandifambe nemi, Tenzi	Let me walk with you, Lord

A theology of a futuristic reward for good behavior functioned very well as an "opiate" in a dictatorial colonial context to keep the dominated group appeased. A dualistic view of existence resulted in a theology of the church that devalued life in the land of the living. In this context salvation meant one's ability to refrain from associating with worldly company and fleshly pursuits. Salvation or freedom meant believers' ability to subdue their fleshly passions and appetites and to aspire to and live only for spiritual nourishment. In the colonial context, for the Methodists, sin meant particular acts, such as drinking, smoking, dancing, and sex.

This early mission church was characterized by a collective spirit of arrogance and self-righteousness on the part of most missionaries. For the most part, the church that had very little time for critical self-examination. Entangled in a web of *quid pro quo* with the colonial systems, the church watered down its message to teaching the laws of the new religion. At the mission one was simply required to observe the do's and don'ts on the issues of dress, etiquette, and habits.[20] New converts were not entrusted with much of a mission except that of bringing others to Christ, which meant helping them to join this community of God's chosen or elect. Any critique of the church or the social status quo was severely sanctioned. Ranger has shown that during this period missionaries monitored and defined the agenda for the Native Minister's Conference. For example, at this Conference native pastors were prohibited from discussing any matters concerning their salaries or State politics.[21]

As a redeemed and redeeming community, the church during these early days largely failed to accomplish its mission of a holistic transformation of individuals and communities with love. Sin, guilt, and repentance became an individualistic and legalistic affair in the Methodist Church. Private confessions and repentance, followed by observance of the law, easily slipped into egocentric exercises in which individuals walked around feeling superior as the elect or harbored self-pride and contempt for the non-Christian community. Such a sense of exclusiveness often betrayed an attitude that regarded others or those outside the church as less than perfect human beings.

The church preached a gospel that esteemed the virtues of poverty, meekness, and chastity to a people and an environment that were under siege. In such an environment, to preach against the love of wealth was tantamount to endorsing a plan for the genocide of a people and their environment. A gospel that chose poverty for the Africans advanced the racist colonial cause by alienating them from their material wealth and heritage, which the church had labeled worldly, fleshly, and evil. It meant that African Christians could no longer take an inventory of resources available for survival. Neither could they seek accountability on how wealth was being acquired and distributed. Even the message of stewardship became irrelevant to a people who were powerless, destitute, and scared.

In cautioning Manyika Christians against the love of material wealth, the church was also creating a community that would accept acute economic disparities within class, race, or gender as normal or natural. Colonial masters were living opulent lifestyles. Even though on a budget, most missionaries lived lifestyles that were far from humble or poor. Missionary budgets were based on the standard of living of the colonial whites in the region. Maintaining a "civilized" lifestyle for its missionaries was part of the church's agenda. As white colonial lifestyle entrenched itself, missionary lifestyles mirrored this material culture in many ways. As part of an upper class, most missionaries hired teams of household servants and felt entitled to such perks and privileges.[22]

For the African Christians, teachers, and ministers, the church either totally forbade or ignored any discussion of the need for an equitable distribution of resources. They were nurtured to be grateful for the little they got and were sometimes reminded that they were not deserving of anything beyond what they were getting. Christians were taught that they should learn frugality and that a little can go very far if good stewardship is practiced. Such messages eventually created a class of people who generally appeared content in what can be termed an environment of "a well-groomed poverty." This is an environment in which individuals and communities manage on meager resources while constantly on the verge of hunger, poverty, or homelessness. In this environment material objects are actually overvalued and viewed as tokens for measuring one's success in the silent war of social classes.

For a long time wealth was put in otherworldly terms for Manyika Christians. Apocalyptic imagery was also conjured up in the theology of these times. Vivid imagery was used to paint a future paradise for Christians. Heaven was a place where the streets were paved in gold and the gates made of pearls and precious stones. In the world to come, evil and the problems of the present would be no more. Believers were being called to passively accept misery on earth while awaiting a paradise—a heaven in which there would be no more pain, tears, or death.

It was not unusual to find many new Christians who had been nursed in this kind of theology viewing this world and existence as evil and therefore regarding anyone with suspicion who sought to engage with it politically or materially. For example, most Christians were very uncomfortable with the idea of getting into business or trade, and those who did were often tormented with rumors and innuendo of having acquired the wealth through evil means.

This chapter began by contrasting two views of the development of Rukwadzano—the official church version and the official version reflecting the development of an authentic and indigenous African expression that grew out of the encounter of a Shona worldview with the gospel. This chapter focused more on the church's version of the development of the woman's organization, while the next two chapters focus on factors leading to the development of the indigenous version.

CHAPTER 6

A New Africa: Transformation

By the 1930s and 1940s the mission church in most parts of Africa except the South was opening a new chapter on its attitudes toward the continent and its people. It was calling for new methods of and attitudes toward doing mission work in Africa. It was also beginning to acknowledge and appreciate Africa's wealth and beauty that had attracted European lust and greed. In his book *Rethinking Africa*, Reverend Henry Nau, a Lutheran U.S.-American missionary to Ibibioland, Nigeria, on most issues writes like a product of his day. But on the issue of African wealth and European and American colonialism he lays out what was happening in very vivid language:

> Rethinking Africa brings us to a consideration of the value of Africa itself. Africa has been considered not worth much as a country [*sic*]. If this were true, why, then, we would ask, have the European nations been so eager to seize every inch of Africa. One needs but to look at the balance sheets of the great United Africa Company, or of John Holt, or of Elder Dempster Line, or Woermann Line, or of the Holland West Africa Line, or of our own American West Africa Line.
>
> On the shore of Senegal colony at Dakar one sees mounts of peanuts waiting for shipment to American and European shores. In Takoradi tons and tons of mica and thousands of mahogany logs wait to be carried to the furniture factories of Europe and America. In the roadways of Accra, at the time of the cocoa harvest, one can count the steamers by the half dozen waiting for their loads. The bright yellow ornaments of the ladies of the Gold coast prove that something more than cocoa gave its name to this part of the coast. See millions of tons of palm oil that month after month find their way into the soap and candle factories of the world, and then again ask the question whether Africa is worth something. The world's greatest copper mines are not in America but Africa. The name Katanga spells copper. The world's diamonds do not come from Amsterdam, but from the mines of South Africa. It is uncertain whether Australia or Africa is the greatest wool

market of the world. Is Africa worth saving? It is the coming rival of our Southern States in cotton trade. It may even gain control of the world market. Egyptian cotton has already won for itself an enviable place.[1]

Such writings from some mission churches were calling for the church to return to its original mandate for the African continent. The church was being called to disembark from the colonial wagon, renounce the lure of lucre, and truly seek to bring good news to the suffering peoples of Africa. Some were calling for new approaches to mission work in an Africa that was becoming free.

Breath of a New Spirit

From 1918 into the 1930s the Methodist Church was experiencing what it called a "Pentecostal" experience at revivals held throughout its missions and outstations. Thus began what may be called the second phase of a faith journey for Africans who had become Christians. This was a time when the African Christians can be said to have come of age. Some of them had accepted the message of the new religion and had read and begun to interpret its scriptures for themselves. Revivals became platforms for personal testimonies of transformation and calls to mission inside and outside the community. It was during this period that Lydia Chimonyo was moved to start a prayer group out of which Rukwadzano grew.

For some missionaries their faith journey was coming full circle—to revival meetings back home in the United States. These missionaries were thrilled because they felt that a time had finally arrived for the church to engage in critical reflection and self-evaluation. Reverend T. A. O'Farrell, the chair at Nyadiri Mission, was one such individual. In a report to the Annual Conference, he expressed with urgency his conviction "that the proper place for a revival to begin is in the hearts of missionaries." Moved by the revival spirit at Nyadiri, he said, the mission closed school for three days for prayer and preaching. During this time a "Pentecostal baptism" occurred in which boys sought confession and prayer counsel and "hearts were laid bare and conversion was experienced." He heard testimony, prayer, and singing like he had never heard before. Praying went on indefinitely and stolen articles were returned. He concluded, "I cannot speak for others; but for myself it surpassed any experience I have ever known. Camp meetings will do it. However, some at Nyadiri have not yet yielded, work is not yet complete."[2]

The Methodist tradition of revivals and camp meetings had once again unleashed a floodgate of diverse claims emerging from personal religious experiences. Suddenly there was cause for alarm when some of its members, like Johanne Marange and Mai Chaza, claimed to have seen visions and to have received a new message and mission for the church. Lydia Chimonyo claimed that she, as a lover of prayer and a strong believer in the power of the Holy Spirit, was looking for women with similar convictions to join her prayer group on campus. The church's concern at this period is well expressed in the report of the Committee on the State of the Church, which called the conference to "warn people against the dangers arising out of the spread of many new and strange doctrines." Leaders were asked to lead people into a deeper spiritual life through teaching them how to pray and how to read the Bible.[3]

Mai Chaza and Johanne Marange eventually left the Methodist Church and founded two of the largest African independent churches in the region—Mai Chaza Church and Vapostori Church. Both churches totally rejected the colonial European worldview and sought to build churches that were tolerant of the African worldview and were willing to acknowledge the suffering of black people under colonial regimes. The liturgy, music, and theological beliefs of these churches were very similar to the unwritten text of the Rukwadzano movement.

Rukwadzano: The Written Text

A general analysis of the written text of Rukwadzano in terms of its constitution and history shows an organization reflecting and replicating the worldview and beliefs of the mission church. First, a theoretical and doctrinal framework was given to ensure that the organization would live by church doctrine. Such a framework was designed primarily to safeguard the power, authority, and influence of the church leadership. Second, the organization's commandments and rules reflected the church's individualistic and legalistic approach to sin, salvation, and vision of the church. One detects very little focus on the Christian message of love, justice, peace, community, and integrity in the written text.

Doctrine and Church Leadership

According to *Rumano* (1938), biblical texts supporting the organization's doctrinal beliefs are Tit. 2:1-15 and 1 Pet. 3:1.[4] An analysis of these texts shows that they uphold the principles and beliefs of the mission church's worldview on gender, race, and class. Both texts give a worldview that is rigidly hierarchical on almost all matters of life. It is a dualistic and hierarchical world in which, for example, wives are to be submissive to their husbands and slaves to their masters. Through the use of these texts the mission church turned a women's religious movement into an organization designed to clone ecclesiastical orthodoxy and in the end indirectly promote the white colonial state.

In this context both texts would serve to endorse as legitimate the power of men over women and that of the white colonial state over the indigenous peoples. For example, 1 Pet. 3:1 begins by admonishing wives to "accept the authority of your husbands, so that even if some of them do not obey the word, they may be won without a word by their wives." Tit. 3:1 reminds believers that they should be "subject to rulers and authorities, to be obedient, to be ready for every good work." On the same theme Titus 2:9 bids "slaves to be submissive to their masters and to give satisfaction in every respect; they are not to talk back, not to pilfer, but to show complete and perfect fidelity, so that in everything they may be an ornament to the doctrine of God our Savior."

Throughout this period the church would endeavor through such teachings to cultivate within its membership non-hostile attitudes toward the colonial government. Ecclesiastical authority continued to rest in the power and authority first of male missionaries, then of their wives, and finally of native clergy. To ensure that the native women's movement could be turned into an "orthodox" organization the church gave it over to the missionary wives. Missionary wives were invested with all the powers and authority to direct and dictate the form, content, and structure of the movement as it was being turned into an organization. Item 10 of the organization's handbook stipulates that there shall be two missionary wives as advisors to the Executive Committee. From this apex missionary wives defined the agenda, formulated policies, and designed the rules and regulations that would run the new organization. Through missionary-wife advisors the mission church was able to continue superimposing Western colonial values, worldview, and doctrinal beliefs. The early structure developed was both hierarchical and autocratic.

Wives of native clergy occupied the second level on this tier of power, authority, and privilege. Most of these women had been educated at the mission and therefore would have been quite conversant with the mission church's worldview. Their authority was exercised at the circuit and local levels. Article 7 of the Handbook stipulated that "the minister's wife alone is empowered to lead the circuit meeting." In addition, all ministers' wives automatically qualified for membership on the Executive Committee. African clergy wives could exercise this power and authority as long as they remembered to defer to their husbands, missionary wives, or male missionaries. In the local church, clergy wives could rule supreme without seeking consensus from membership.

Membership

On the question of who could become a member, the constitution states, "All women and older girls who are full members of the Methodist Church may be received as members of the Rukwadzano. Probationers (in church relation) may not enter into full membership of the Society."[5] Reading from this early draft on the subject of membership, one would assume it was pretty much open to all women who were full members of the church. However, two features evolved to become definitive on admission into membership. First, because the term *older girls* does not stipulate at what age a girl could be regarded as older, very few "older girls" ever qualified for admission into the organization. Second, the emphasis and focus by the mission church on a Christian marriage for African women soon became the criterion by which a woman's character and commitment to the church were judged. A Christian marriage became the necessary requirement admission into the organization. The early mission church, with the support of the missionary wives, not only promoted Christian marriage as the panacea to the indigenous woman's social problems but also strongly held nineteenth-century doctrinal beliefs that viewed women as holier and more religious than men. A woman in a Christian marriage was considered a vital channel of "salvation" for her husband and children. Women were entrusted with the duty of living exemplary lives for the sake of their husbands and children.

The Society's constitution nowhere stipulates that a Christian marriage was required for admission into the organization, but existing in an environment in which this issue was on the agenda of every annual conference of the Methodist Episcopal Church, the Society soon considered Christian marriage a membership requirement.

Christian Marriage

In the written text of Rukwadzano, a Christian marriage was given as the ultimate solution to emancipating the African woman, who was cast as a victim of indigenous customs and practices. African women were viewed as beasts of burden who were bought and sold into polygamous marriages. A Christian marriage was an arrangement that would guarantee the African woman a monogamous relationship and the right to join a culture and civilization that, in terms of work, required nothing of her beyond motherhood and domestic work.[6]

The church marketed a Christian marriage as a requirement that not only enhanced the status of a Manyika woman but also ushered in a world of leisure and luxury for the young woman. A Manyika woman could also become a "Victorian Lady." In this world, she could stay home and have every need and want provided for by her husband while, as the mistress of her household, she managed a fleet of servants and all affairs pertaining to it. In an environment where colonial culture was self-validating, whites did not consider such a world and such imagery as utopian. It was a world where white men exploited every resource in sight in order to provide for their women, who stayed at home managing a fleet of servants. However, at this stage, it was still utopian for Africans. Marriage perhaps symbolized the meeting point of the mission church and colonial culture. Colonial culture and mission church became one in this outward expression in terms of style in dress, ceremony, and reception. On this occasion, garbed in Western colonial splendor, a young woman could be made to feel that the utopian dream of leisure and "class" was finally within her grasp. After the wedding a young Christian couple was expected to live the lifestyle of a "civilized" (European/Western) family as well as follow the colonial capitalist dream. For example, in the early Conference minutes, pastor-teachers and evangelists were constantly reminded to live model lifestyles in terms of housing, diet, and dress for all to see. Pastors' wives were urged to learn hygiene, housekeeping, dressmaking, and all domestic arts thoroughly.[7]

The mission church shared very little of its doctrinal understanding of a Christian marriage. Upon a Christian marriage a young Manyika woman entered a world in which she and her relationships were redefined according to the church's interpretation of certain scriptural texts. A Christian marriage became the major requirement for entrance into the Women's Society because of the church's understanding of this event. The Protestant mission church groomed all its young women to view marriage as the culminating event or ultimate achievement of their lives. Upon marriage a woman assumed personal responsibility not only for her own loyalty to the Christian faith but also for that of her husband and her children.

On female sexuality the church gave a double message typical of Victorian culture. In the texts Rukwadzano used, women were clearly portrayed as the "weaker sex" (1 Pet. 3:7), depicted as more prone than men to sexual temptation. Yet in the same texts, women in marriage are entrusted with the moral responsibility of leading their husbands and children to salvation (1 Pet. 3:2). Women could accomplish this task only through being submissive to their husbands and heeding the advice of older women and church leaders.

Young women were socialized to view the preservation of one's virginity as the litmus test for one's holiness. A girl's failure to preserve her virginity was tantamount to eternal condemnation. In such a state a young woman was considered dangerous and unredeemable. For the young woman who had preserved her chastity the reward or honor was to be asked into a Christian marriage by a young man through a "white wedding" (white dress). Virginity was the ultimate gift she offered to the man she was marrying. She would offer herself as a blemish-free sacrificial lamb. The color *white* symbolized purity in the church's worldview. On this occasion the girl, literally like a queen, wore the bridal crown on her head, symbolizing victory over all sexual temptation. On this day the girl was supposed to experience bliss as if she had entered the Christian heaven. However, the young man wore black, a color that in the mission church's view of the world usually symbolized sin and vice but in this context signified solemnity.

After a girl sacrificed her virtue through a Christian marriage, the church continued to project female sexuality as the point at which women could be either saved or condemned. Upon marriage a young woman was further asked to remain chaste and reverent in behavior by submitting to her husband. Titus 2 urges young women "to love their husbands, to love their children, to be self-controlled, chaste, good managers of the household, kind, being submissive to their husbands, so that the word of God may not be discredited." The solution to this women's condition is that they be submissive to their husbands. The advice for women to become agents of salvation is not that they just be submissive to their husbands but also that they not be consumed with outward appearance such as "braiding your hair, and by wearing gold ornaments or fine clothing; rather, let your adornment be the inner self with the lasting beauty of a gentle and quiet spirit, which is very precious in God's sight" (1 Pet. 3:3).

Through the yoke of a Christian marriage, a woman was then portrayed as stronger than man in matters pertaining to human salvation. By self-emptying and submission to male authority a woman attained the ability to redeem both herself and others. According to church thought, there was no hope of or guarantee for a woman's and humanity's salvation outside of a Christian marriage. This is why a Christian marriage became mandatory for admission into the Society. This practice, however, is not consistent with the official policy of the Society. That policy states that membership is open to "all women and older girls who are full members of the Methodist Church."[8]

Rules and Regulations

Members of the Society were to live by certain rules and regulations. Failure to comply with these meant suspension or automatic disqualification. The rules and regulations of Rukwadzano reflect the doctrinal beliefs of both the Society and the mission church. Rules and regulations were designed to guide women to live out their faith consistent with sound church doctrine. An analysis of these rules and regulations shows a church perpetuating a colonial worldview in which women were coerced into what became similar to a cult of motherhood and were relegated to the domestic sphere. For example, of Rukwadzano's ten rules, the first seven are devoted either to stating that all domestic work is a woman's duty or to renouncing the fundamentals of Shona culture and embracing a "Christian civilization" way of life. There is no mention of a woman's need to participate beyond the household sphere in any manner. The rules are patterned after the Maternal Societies of nineteenth-century Western Christianity.[9]

Domestic Rules

A woman's duties around the house are defined in three areas. First, a woman is expected to devote herself to motherhood. Second, she is assigned to housekeeping and, third, to taking care of her husband. All these duties are included in the list of duties required of a Rukwadzano member as follows: Teach her children Christian customs; dress her children adequately; keep her home and children clean; look after her husband's clothes, keeping them clean and the buttons sewed on; and give him warm water with which to bathe.[10]

With such a dogmatic duty assigned to women, the church through the organization started a social and economic revolution. It was at this point that the Manyika women exchanged a hoe for a broom.

A new image of womanhood was created for Rukwadzano women. Limited to the domestic sphere, women were being groomed to become ladies in the European, Victorian manner. They were taught and nurtured to keep themselves, their houses, and their children clean and pretty in order to please their husbands. To treat her husband as her master and to provide for his every need and comfort was a woman's duty. Women were sold the colonial capitalist dream that one day their husbands would become wealthy and they could finally acquire all what was needed to live a "Christian lifestyle." Women were to put their husbands and family first at all times. They were also taught that it was through their example that both the children and their husbands could live lives of faith (1 Pet. 3:1).

Uniform

In 1934, the organization started off with a red and blue badge with an insignia for membership. The badge was designed by Mrs. Murphree. Ten years later a uniform was designed. The constitution gives a brief history of the origin of the uniform and its symbolism.

> While at a Dumba meeting at Old Mutare in 1948, they thought of having an R.R.W. uniform, which is used up to now. This uniform was to be different from other types of dresses. The dress is blue, representing the color of the badge. The hem of the arms, belt and collar is red, representing the blood which cleansed us. The head gear is white cloth showing that we have been cleansed. Mrs. Murphree gave us the collar pattern.
>
> Members are expected to wear uniform when attending the following: 1. The Lord's Supper; 2. Meetings of Rukwadzano (regular and official); 3. To the funeral of a Christian, and 4. Revival meetings of the Rukwadzano, of the *Vabvuwi* (Methodist Men) or of the M.Y.F.[11]

The idea of a uniform may have been inspired by the desire to express solidarity with and to live out the scriptural tenets that called them to dress simply and to renounce the trappings of outward adornment.

There are three issues of concern regarding the uniform of the organization. First, the colors and the symbolism of the uniform were not only foreign to the Manyika worldview but also were the colors of the national flag of the country from which the Methodist missionaries had come—the United States. Second, a uniform in the colonial context may have been an additional tool of control that served to stifle women's spirit of creativity. Third, the uniform at times became a symbol of the church's pietistic and elitist attitude toward nonmembers or those who had "failed" by the group's standards.

Red, white, and blue colors for a Manyika women's organization may have been of no more significance than a lack of imagination on the part of Mrs. Murphree, the American missionary woman/wife who suggested the colors. Yet, the repercussions of such a choice went much deeper. Not only does the color symbolism of the U.S. national flag evoke sentiments of patriotism and a shared history with a particular national group of people but, in the era of colonialism such as the late-nineteenth and early-twentieth centuries, these colors of a national flag also came to symbolize a foreign nation's conquest and dominant presence among a people. The colors of a flag were a symbol of the foreign power's superimposing its whole worldview upon a people of another culture through military force or coercion. After having been allowed into a country by a colonial power, this nation could, through religion and education, exert all the influence necessary to superimpose its worldview on a conquered people.[12]

The suggestion to use the colors of the American flag for the uniforms of Manyika women converts made them associate these colors with a religious significance. The colors of the flag evoked sentiments of the holy and the sacred, purity, and the blood of Christ.

The colors red, white, and blue identified Rukwadzano women as different, as redeemed and clean/pure. One's wearing of these colors was therefore viewed as a matter of profound significance. A woman who aspired to wear these colors had to go through the show of a Christian marriage, pledge to search for holiness, and show piety through living for her children and husband. If a woman failed to meet these requirements, she was never admitted into the organization. For example, during the installation service for a new member, one of the questions the minister asked was this: "Do you promise to live a good life, of self-denial, faithful, and righteous in all things?" The new member responded with the following promise, "I promise before God, that I shall keep all the laws of the Rukwadzano. If I break them, I shall return my badge (and uniform) to the chairman."[13]

This kind of symbolism attached to one's wearing the uniform promoted a self-righteous and elitist attitude related to nonmembers and non-Christians. Some women in the church, even after a Christian marriage, felt they would never attain the degree of piety or holiness required to be admitted to or to remain in the organization. Those unmarried women who were full members of the church were made to feel inadequate and irresponsible by failing to "lure their husbands to the altar for a Christian marriage." Together with older single and divorced women, they were made to feel that a woman could not be saved outside of a Christian marriage. The uniform came to symbolize the Rukwadzano rules and regulations that implicitly groomed its membership to be exclusive, arrogant, and self-righteous.

Even when one became a member, there was no guarantee of one's staying a member. The rules and regulations were often either too broad or too specific as well as gender biased. For example, while telling women to teach children what are termed but not specified as "Christian customs," the rules also broadly reject all of Manyika culture by forbidding certain practices such as the brewing of beer or the use of what is termed as "evil medicine."[14] Women are further instructed not to "smoke tobacco" or "work in the fields of tobacco," a rule that would later become impossible for women to abide by in their search for survival in a colonial economy that introduced the growing of tobacco as one of the primary commercial agricultural schemes.

An extremely sensitive aspect of the self-righteousness of Rukwadzano rules lay in the "defrocking" of a member of her uniform because her daughter had become pregnant outside of a Christian marriage. Since a Rukwadzano woman had been invested with and had accepted the responsibility of raising her children in a Christian way, she was in turn held totally accountable for anything perceived as having gone wrong. A daughter's getting pregnant outside of a Christian marriage was considered the deadliest of sins or ultimate evidence that a Rukwadzano mother had not done her duty well. This unwritten rule represented the epitome of the church's gender bias against women and their faith and sexuality. In this case the church was using women to control other women's sexuality through punishment and rejection. In Rukwadzano those women whose daughters got pregnant out of wedlock were punished by stripping them of their uniform; and the daughters were ostracized, rejected, and made to feel unwelcome at church. The children they bore could not be baptized in the church.[15]

Such a situation was a far cry from Shona culture, which referred to the pregnancy of a young woman or any woman as *anaka* ("she has attained beauty").[16] On the other hand, the colonial situation was no longer an environment where anything was guaranteed. Mothers and fathers suddenly had to be legitimately concerned about their daughters in an environment that was promoting sexism, male arrogance, dominance, and unaccountability. In Western colonial culture, specifically in Zimbabwe and southern Africa, it was acceptable for a young or older man to deceive, rape, or seduce a young woman and reject any commitment or responsibility the woman or community asked of him. Such behavior was very rare in Manyika culture, where such situations often met with grave consequences for the man involved.

Rukwadzano women were desperately seeking to protect their children, especially girls, from the ultimate colonial curse—getting pregnant. In this culture a girl who got pregnant and was rejected by the lover had no place to seek refuge. If in school, she was immediately dismissed, and if at home (a Christian home), she would be chased away. Except for very limited positions in the domestic sector, she could not find a job in the colonial system. Even when she found a job, there was no accommodation for her child. In the process of seeking to protect their daughters from the curse and scourge of out-of-wedlock pregnancies Rukwadzano women ended up looking as if they were the agents of colonial and mission-church sexist ideology that sought to control all aspects of women's sexuality.

Finally, not only were the uniform and its colors foreign to Manyika women—as tools used to express group solidarity and commitment to a simple way of living—but in the colonial context the church also used them to control both the bodies and the minds of women. If one wore the uniform, as in the military, one would be expected to live by the doctrine, rules, and regulations as well; failing to do so caused one to face grave consequences. As members, women would not be in a position to initiate or create much, given the organization's hierarchy of structure and uniformity in dress. Such a situation would have been rife for creating dictatorial leaders and a silent and lethargic membership.

Materially, the uniform also indirectly aided the colonial schemes of economic dispossession and deprivation. Through the use of biblical texts, such as 1 Pet. 3, the church insisted women renounce their material culture in terms of beauty and dress and jewelry fashion. Women were admonished against the use of these with the general explanation that they are symbols of female vanity. For example, in the Annual Conference Minutes, the Committee on the State of the Church advised that the Manyika custom of young men giving expensive gifts to their girlfriends or fiancées should be stopped. Yet the idea of a uniform that included head coverings and forbade cosmetic make-up or jewelry alienated women from their material culture. A dualistic worldview in which they were taught to despise material culture as evil and vain was an underlying theme of the wearing of a uniform. A majority of the Manyika women culti-vated very strict and conservative tastes in dress and style for their daughters. On the other hand, European colonialists were nurturing their daughters in a hedonistic culture, teaching them that it was proper to expect expensive gifts from their boyfriends or fiancées.

The written text of *Rumano* (1938) shows a mission church that sought to control the religious and social lives of Manyika women through the imposition of an organizational structure and repressive doctrinal rules and regulations. However, in this harsh colonial environment, the mission church had sown the seeds of a message of compassion, sacrifice, healing, liberation, and community—that is, the message of Jesus Christ.

After reading, studying, and listening to the Scriptures in their own context, the seeds of this message began to take root in women like Lydia Chimonyo. With faith, courage, and conviction, these women responded to a call to mission communicated through an "unwritten text" lying behind the official text of the Rukwadzano movement.

CHAPTER 7

Rukwadzano: The Unwritten Text

FROM THE BEGINNING AN UNWRITTEN TEXT LAY BEHIND THE BIRTH AND DEVELopment of this women's group in the Methodist Episcopal Church. An analysis of Rukwadzano shows that it became both a movement and an organization that functioned through the beliefs and application of both written and unwritten texts from two worldviews. Underneath mission-church orthodoxy lay a Manyika movement that both informed and continued to draw from the indigenous worldview on matters of faith and salvation.

In the zeal of forcing Christianity down the throats of a people, the mission church often began by desecrating the Shona sacred places. The church either cleared the area or buried their dead in areas the Shona considered sacred. For example, Bernard Mizeki, a missionary of the Anglican Church, angered the Mangwende people by clearing one of their most sacred areas for a garden. He did this despite pleas and angry protests from every side asking him to leave the area undisturbed. The individuals who murdered him during the uprising always cited this act of Mikezi's as the reason for his murder. Cecil John Rhodes requested to be buried at the Matombo, one of the most sacred shrines of the Shona and Ndebele.

The Methodists were following the same tradition when choosing sites for holding their camp meetings in the 1920s and 1930s. Here is a description on the Nyatande Camp Meeting site:

> God will satisfy a hungry heart anywhere, but Nyatande is an ideal spot in which to find Him. The camp is situated on a slightly elevated piece of land between two rivers which flow parallel. In fact, it is a perfect place for a village, and the missionaries could at first understand why it had been left for so long, while the surrounding villages had been built in much less advantageous spots. Finally the reason was found.

There was an old superstition that this particular elevation was inhabited by the spirits. It had been named, "The hill of the Spirits," and the Natives were afraid to live there. So this place was avoided by the heathen people all through the years, and now the "Hill of the Spirits" has been set aside for Camp Meeting use. Now instead of evil spirits, the Spirit of God is meeting with the people there. One Native man expressed the feeling of the Christians about Nyatande when he said, "I think that God knew that sometime there would be a Camp Meeting here, and so He made this place and has kept it all these years for this purpose."[1]

Places like the Nyatande campground could be symbolic of the irony of the founding, nature, and development of the church in Manyikaland and in Zimbabwe generally. Christianity chose to superimpose itself by literally grabbing some of the Shona religious shrines and converting them to its use. One would think that after such a bold step, the church would rest assured it had "slain the dragons." However, the church soon realized it was not just at these shrines where these "evil spirits" lay. At revival meetings held in the 1930s and 1940s some of its native members were coming up with "strange doctrine." And these strange doctrines resembled indigenous beliefs.

For a majority of African converts, beneath the veneer of mission-church doctrinal orthodoxy lay a deep, seething spirituality steeped in the traditional worldview waiting to explode. This phenomenon came to a head and manifested itself in the Methodist Episcopal Church when members like Johanne Marange and Mai Chaza arose preaching "new" messages about redemption and healing. On his message of redemption, Johanne Marange was to leave the church and found one of the earliest and largest African independent churches in the region. Mai Chaza wished to stay in the Methodist church to practice her healing ministry, but the church declined her wish. She went on to found the Mai Chaza Church. Centered around her healing ministry, the church has flourished in Zimbabwe.[2]

During this period, Lydia Chimonyo founded her prayer group among African ministers' wives at Old Mutare mission. From this prayer group Rukwadzano emerged. According to *Rumano* (1944), the biggest question for the mission was whether or not to allow this prayer group to continue. The church was suspicious of the time, circumstances, message, and messenger in the leadership of Lydia Chimonyo. *Rumano* underscores that the texts from which Lydia Chimonyo is said to have claimed to draw authority to do her work— Tit. 2:1; 1 Pet. 3:1—show that they were either superimposed on her by the mission church or she gave these texts as her sources in order to silence mission church opposition to her prayer group. In citing these texts as authoritative sources for her work, Lydia Chimonyo was able to remain in the church and lead the prayer group that was soon organized by the church through women missionaries. On the other hand, the church had decided not to continue losing its membership to the "new and strange" doctrines but to keep any suspicious elements in check through teaching, missionary supervision, and organization.

Manyika Worldview

Underneath the mission church's written text Lydia Chimonyo had laid a foundation with elemental beliefs and a structure that reflected the Manyika worldview. Themes of this unwritten text would run beneath and be recognizable throughout the birth, growth, and development of Rukwadzano. Beneath the mission church's organization of its church women lay a movement of Manyika women who had converted to Christianity. Manyika women had forged a movement that reconciled the biblical religion to their worldview despite the context of colonization. In this way, the movement very much resembled the African independent churches being founded by individuals breaking away from mission churches all over the region. African independent churches were looking for a Christian church they could call home. They were looking for a church that not only could accepted the fundamentals of the African worldview but also acknowledged the hurt of a people in colonial bondage. From its birth, nature, and development, the unwritten text of Rukwadzano was grounded in the Shona worldview.

Birth

Lydia Chimonyo started her base community prayer group by inviting women who loved praying. This community chose space outside the mission for meeting, out in the forest where they would go while pretending to be gathering fuel wood. Here the women were free to open up and name their innermost thoughts in a non-bounded space. As pastor-teacher's wives women might have begun to realize that their power and influence were often marginal in relation to the established church at the mission. From the meeting in the forest, they chose a time to meet and selected sites for the rendezvous. Both the time and the sites for meeting were marginal, that is, outside of the mission grounds and agenda.

Meeting for prayer at 4:00A.M. is significant in the Shona worldview. Around this time *masambanzou* ("the time in which elephants bathe") is believed to be the time when the human can transcend all constraints and attain oneness with the universe. In this state the human is able to secure information and inspiration on how to live or continue surviving in difficult times. *Mashambazhou* is the time when humans can clear their chests, empty selves, be one with the universe, and commune with God and the ancestors—an experience from which they will draw wisdom, peace, and strength to go on. A member was expected to observe this hour of prayer daily, by herself or in the community of other members.

The prayers said at this time were spontaneous. Individual women took turns to pray and a prayer lasted for as long as the woman felt like praying. During this time, the other members in the group would respond in affirmation or acclamation. Only song was allowed to interrupt or intersperse prayer. Prayer was (and still is) central to the worldview of the movement in that it was perceived as a democratic exercise in which the individual heard herself and was heard by the community. It was during these prayer exercises that the group identified members who had special needs, concerns, or problems and proceeded to find ways of alleviating the various situations. Rukwadzano also believed that during these prayer exercises individuals in a trance state might attain the capabilities of discerning any special gifts they had for their own good or for the good of the community.

Sites

As in the case with African independent church groups, the prayer group movement selected two sites outside mission grounds and designated them as holy. Johanne Marange chose a site south of Mutare and named it *Jerusalem Itsva* ("The New Jerusalem"), where all the followers were to come on pilgrimage in search of wisdom, peace, strength, and prosperity. Mai Chaza chose a site outside Harare in Seke and named it *Guta raJehova* ("the City of God"), where her healing ministry was centered. Rukwadzano selected two sites, one in the east, which they called *paDara* ("the watchtower") and one in the west, which they called *paChingando* ("the place of deep meditation/transcendental thoughts").

The names of the prayer sites are significant. First, there is paDara, by which the women were signifying that the times were calling for a people to be on watch because their very survival had been threatened. On the watchtower they also felt confident that they could call upon God to come for their redemption. Lydia Chimonyo and her community were calling upon God to free them from what they defined as "earthly troubles."[3] The mission church was teaching them that they needed God to save them from the "darkness" of their skin, flesh, culture, and environment. It was at these new locations that the women claimed the prophetic tradition of the Christian faith and began to act as the "voices crying in the wilderness" for the church and political system to do what was right. They were being led to embrace the heart of the Christian message while at the same time embracing themselves and their cultural traditions.

At paChingando, through chant and prayer, women expected to empty themselves of all anger, resentment, strife, anxiety, and hurt. They expected to be healed and to acquire wisdom on issues of survival. Women were in search of a community, a message and a voice that heals. Such a thing was not to be found in the mission church of their day. At mission hospitals the church was healing the personal physical wounds, but it was oblivious to the corporate pain and suffering of a people under the racist colonial domination. At paChingando women found redemption; they could go back to the mission and home no longer as victims but as wholesome agents of change for building a new community.

Sin and Salvation

According to *Rumano* (1944), the group led by Lydia Chimonyo was searching to be "free from earthly troubles."[4] Such an understanding of sin and evil stems from the Shona worldview. In his book *Bantu Philosophy*, Tempels presented a plausible exposition of Bantu philosophical theology that includes that of the Shona.[5] Tempels asserts that Bantu philosophy begins and ends with the relationship between the Creator Being (*Mwari*) and the Created Beings (*Munhu Zvinhu*). This relationship is crucial to the created beings because the Creator is the source of life or vital energy. The source of personal happiness (*munhu*) is the divinely given energy, or vital energy. The freedom to enjoy one's life energy is for the human being a reason for existence. Being born in a healthy community, an individual can be nurtured to recognize, cherish, and affirm the life force in others through wholesome relationships.

Munhu's vital energy is in relation not only to the Creator or other humans but also to the whole of creation. All creation has life energy in relation to one another. Human beings are nurtured through the Mutupo principle to recognize and affirm the life-energy in animals, rocks, trees, rivers, and spaces. This is why Rukwadzano and African independent churches insist on worshiping out-of-doors—under a tree, by a large rock or a river, or in a forest—to seek oneness with nature. Before or after the killing of any animal for food or ritual, the Shona traditionally offer a sorrowful prayer to the animal's life energy and to the Creator in explanation of the act. Beings are understood as intimately bonded to one another in such a way that their influence on each other can weaken or strengthen the other's vital energy.

A fundamental aspect of the Shona worldview on evil is that good and bad are not understood in terms of reward and punishment. Individuals are not motivated to do good for the sake of immediate or future reward or punishment. One is good in this life simply because one is expected to be so. In turn, one expects everyone else to be good and diligently to commit himself or herself to relationships that guarantee happiness and a future in existence. The reward for goodness in Shona worldview is one's own and the community's vitality. In this worldview, health (*Utanu*) in the land of the living is the reward for corporate goodness.

When suffering, pain, or disease invades an individual, it is named evil and the community sets to identify the source of it. Shonas would not search for an imaginary force outside the community to identify as the source of suffering. Instead, they analyze every act or being of those in a relational context, seeking to identify the point at which a relationship became "evil" and how it could be restored to goodness. The community cooperates in investigating the source of suffering, pain, or death; and it is also the community that determines the nature of the remedy necessary to heal the hurt.

Further, the Shona worldview generally holds evil, suffering, and disease as primarily of human origin. Humans are understood to possess the will to choose to exercise their vital energy to positively or negatively influence the other in whatever way they act. Specific acts by individuals or groups that choose to violate a community's norms create disharmony and deplete its happiness. Such disruptive human behavior ranges from political injustice and incest to simply uttering a word of insult to one's neighbor or a stranger. For example, in Shona society individuals refrain from any form of angry verbal exchange, because if one party in such an exchange falls sick or dies soon after, the other party cannot deny accusations of witchcraft (*Uroyi*).

On the issue of sin and guilt, the Shona worldview requires that when an individual or group has committed sin or violated a norm it is imperative that they rectify the situation through repentance and reparation. They are required to restore harmony and equilibrium to the entity violated. This process involves both the individual and the community. It seeks to ensure that the violator and the victim, as well as the community, are healed and restored. In this context sin, guilt, and forgiveness are not an individual affair between a person and the deity but involve the community of the living, the dead, and the deity. One cannot turn directly to the Creator Being before rectifying and seeking forgiveness from the community. Public and private repentance and penance are demanded if one is considered to be truly seeking forgiveness. The community administers the ritual for the absolution of guilt after one has shown repentance through penance and restoration of a situation by reparations.[6]

When there is disease, death, or any other form of suffering, the community cannot go on until the source of evil has been located. Since evil or sin robs the community and individuals of vital energy, happiness, or peace, going on with business as usual is perceived as a threat to the whole community, women and men, young and old, nature and animals. When the individual suffers, the whole community suffers. Priests, prophets, healers, leaders, and teachers are then entrusted with the responsibility of locating the source of evil and prescribing the balm that can heal a community and its land. Since such collective evil is understood as witchcraft, this involves hunting for and expunging the sources of the witchery.[7]

The Shona worldview focused on creating and sustaining a healing community on earth. Paradise was not simply a future ideal but was an existence that a community could aspire to in the land of the living. Heaven was not a futuristic special location where the righteous went after they died but rather a living reality made possible by the whole community of the Creator and the created, the living and the dead, the neighbor and the stranger together. Each person in the community was expected to play his or her part in seeking to promote harmony and healing the wounds of those who hurt. In such a worldview there is no dualism between medicine and religion, flesh and spirit, man or woman, religion or politics, young or old. All such distinctions become one in a community that is healthy and whole.

The Rukwadzano understanding of sin and redemption was born

out of the unwritten text of the Shona worldview. While seeking to be free "from earthly troubles," these women were not praying to die. Rather, they were seeking to live in a world free of any evil force that had descended upon the land. Drawing from Shona tradition, they set to found a community that could be prophetic as well as committed to works of comforting and healing a hurting community.

The women started by ministering among themselves through exercises of healing in prayer and song. As in the African independent church tradition, women continued the Shona custom of using music and chant to invoke the center of all of reality as community. Rukwadzano music and dance, even when drawn from the Methodist hymnal, picked up traditional Shona music of a people wailing to God to be saved. As the prayer meeting went on, they were known to delve into purely Shona traditional chants of a people in crisis:

Ha Ha Ha!	Ha Ha Ha!
Ndoita seiko Mambo!	What do I do now, God?
Ishe Wangu!	O My God!
Ha Woye Woye!	(cry for help)
Huyai Mundionerewo!	Come and see for yourself!
Is he Wangu!	My God!
Dze Dze Dze!	(a weary and faintwalk)
Muchinjiko wacho Kurema!	This cross is too heavy to carry!

Some of these lyrics and music were too complex for missionaries to decipher. However, missionaries were always able to caution the women against "real dancing." At their revival meetings women built booths and shelters by themselves and eventually invited the male group (*Vabvuwi*) to join them. At such a gathering, they sang together the music and danced the dance of a suffering people. Rukwadzano liturgy, music, and prayer at their informal gatherings expressed the pain and frustration of a people in bondage. It was during these kinds of worship services that women preached a Christian message that converted even some of the indigenous political leadership, such as Ishe Gandanzara, who decided to become a Christian during Martha Chikosi's preaching in August 1933.[8] They were in search of a healing community that could in turn heal others. They were seeking to be delivered, to be redeemed from the grip of an evil system, a racist colonial domination. Eventually, traditional Shona dancing and the evocation of the Mutupos of each group present would be introduced at the revival meetings, deepening the use of Shona culture.

In the meantime women in the different prayer communities focused on healing each other so they could heal their families and communities. Drawing from the Shona past, community arose at local and national levels. Healers, politicians, sages, prophets, and counselors—all practiced their ministry in the community and outside the community, whenever called upon to do so. These women, as in Shona culture, were bold and comfortable with their mission and calling. The church would seek to "tame" these initiatives by superimposing its rigid, hierarchical structure in the form of the 1938 formal organization of the movement. But this would not stop the women, who by then had developed a reputation for speaking their minds in search of justice and were therefore generally feared by the established hierarchy; that is, missionaries, their wives, and native clergy.

At prayer services women sought healing in personal as well as social matters. Here women had a space where their issues were important and not marginal. African women's issues could be treated with urgency, a source of pain and suffering could be identified and remedied, and a reparation or a solution could be applied. For example, in case of stress or anxiety a woman was nursed back to a healthy mind by using all available approaches, such as counseling, prayer, exorcism, and companionship. Those with fertility problems were not ignored but were offered hope through prayer and Shona customary or Western ways of child adoption.

Healing

Most Rukwadzano exercises and activities centered on healing. The concepts of this word were drawn from the Shona worldview. In this worldview health was considered most vital to happiness. One's well-being, or health, reflected that everything around one was at peace. Their total environment was at peace. As mentioned earlier, in case of an illness, pain, or suffering, the community was to use all means at its disposal to diagnose the source of pain and to seek remedy for restoring health.[9]

Women attended the revival meetings primarily for two reasons. First, they came to hear the message as interpreted by their own leaders and, second, they came to heal. At these gatherings, the greatest preacher among them preached all day, interrupted only by music, dance, and prayer. The healing services took place at night. Male clergy and missionaries usually retired to sleep in the evening. After the evening sermon and prayer an announcement would be made letting the women know that the rest of the night, until morning, was devoted to *MaPaka* (derived from "park"), small-group-meeting healing services. These were voluntary. Women who were healthy and at peace usually celebrated life in song and prayer all night around a fire. Around this fire one heard endless witnessing, prayer, song, dance, and cries for freedom, justice, and peace.

Each group was "staffed" by individuals or leaders who were gifted in different areas of healing, such as physical illnesses, fear, anger, infertility, hurt, victims of hatred, stress, divorce, abandonment, bereavement, pride, or simply unhappiness. A woman would also choose whether or not to join a group from her home community. The leaders always advised women to heal in the home-community context when family counseling was needed.

Those designated as leaders were selected not because they were literate elites but, as in Shona worldview, because they were gifted and kind or were good listeners. The group identified such individuals regardless of their age. At the service, the one gifted in music would lead with the appropriate music for the group. As in a Shona traditional religious service, the call and response music style was sung and played all through the session. The volume and intensity of the music were regulated spontaneously as the healing session went on. Music and dance are channels for meditative healing in Shona ritual because through them the individual can come to a dynamic consciousness of himself or herself, the deity, the community, and his or her environment.

A leader might highlight the issues around the "hurt" they were dealing with and the women were assured that they were at a place for healing. Women were free to participate in any way in the service—pray, sing, dance, meditate or talk to themselves or to someone else. Each woman was made to feel her life, pain, freedom, grief, and happiness. The climactic healing moments occurred in the early morning hours. Leaders administered individual laying-on of hands. The chanting did not stop. An observer would usually hear wailings and moaning and witness members being held still due to uncontrollable convulsions. For some members the healing process was not so "violent" an affair.

Praxis

At the revival meeting the leadership always underscored that it was critical for all members to be healed because there was work out there to do. A key theme in Rukwadzano messages was that Christianity calls individuals first to be transformed and healed and then to assist others in receiving the healing they have received. Every member was called upon to go back to her community and live exemplary lives. They were called to seek to create happy communities in spite of the evil grip of colonial domination.

When a death, divorce, or illness occurred in the local communities, Rukwadzano women ministered to each other. Local groups performed household chores for each other and continued to care for an individual in need until she recovered. Rukwadzano also visited the sick at home and in the hospitals. They offered financial support to nonmembers in the community who were sick, destitute, poor, or in crisis. Many of these women became youth counselors in the local church and civic organizations.

They met for prayer, business, and consultation every Friday. After prayer, women learned arts and crafts and sold items for fundraising projects or individual earning. In this context women shared a space free from oppressive and repressive dominance. Rukwadzano reminded them that they were "invincible" and was there to enable them continually to stay in that space against all odds.

Politicians and Social Activists

By the 1960s and 1970s, other dimensions of the Manyika worldview erupted when Rukwadzano demanded direct involvement in two affairs considered public and political. First, they called for a review of government and mission-school admissions practices for gender bias against young girls. Meanwhile with very limited financial, professional, and human resources they decided to propose to the government that they build their own school for girls. Second, during this latter period Rukwadzano shattered the mission-church tenet of seeking separation between church and state and delved into the political arena against the all-white Ian Smith regime.

Historically the church and government recruited and admitted very few girls for further education.[10] The situation did not improve with time. Rukwadzano pointed out that the plight of these young girls/women upon leaving primary school was becoming more and more acute. Places for further education or employment were not available.[11]

A vast number of these young women became victims of rape or deception. Most of them survived marginally and languished in poverty or idleness. Their only way out was to marry a young man who was gainfully employed and thus to become a housewife. In desperate attempts to marry such young men a vast number of these young women fell victim to deception.

Those who left for urban areas in search of jobs were often under-employed as domestic servants in dubious arrangements where they were vulnerable to rape and abuse. Some of these young women resorted to prostitution in search of "easier" means of survival. It was during this period that the resounding chorus at Rukwadzano meetings and prayer vigils, *"Vana Vedu, Vana Vedu"* ("We mourn for the plight of our children"), was most popular. In 1968, Rukwadzano garnered all its meager resources and made a proposal to the government that it be allowed to open a high school for girls. The government approved the proposal but stipulated that under its system the new school would not meet the criteria to qualify for a high school but would be classified as an "F2," or industrial training school.

Rukwadzano accepted this arrangement; hired faculty and a woman principal; selected a site at Mutambara, southeast of Mutare; and named the school Sunny Side.

Rukwadzano raised money to operate the school and pay subsidies toward faculty salaries and student scholarships. The curriculum for the new school offered a general education with special emphasis on home economics. Here, the young girls could at least buy time as they figured out what to do with their lives. The idea was so successful that the government later picked it up and opened F2 schools all over the country. *Wabvuwi* (the Methodist men's church group) followed Rukwadzano's example and opened a boys' school at Nyadiri mission, northeast of Harare.

Politics

Rukwadzano increasingly found itself in a political environment whose relentless tyranny was escalating. Their songs and prayers of remembering and yearning for Zion were moving them to action. The 1960s and 1970s saw a full-blown participation of women in the area the mission church called politics, an area the church traditionally prohibited its members from associating with. Rukwadzano had entered, never to turn back.

Throughout this period the order of the day was turmoil and unrest. The Rhodesian government was employing its strongest measures to silence opposition and keep what it termed "law and order." For one to show open political defiance was tantamount to declaration of war, meaning military combat with the government. Nationalist parties, their leadership, and organizers were being banned, persecuted, or detained. The Rukwadzano women in rural and urban centers organized open defiance campaigns. They were persecuted, arrested, and detained in government crackdowns.[12]

Such government actions did not intimidate the women's resolve openly to demand freedom and civil rights. In the 1970s Rukwadzano women marched and demonstrated against the banning of the Bishop of the Methodist Church, Abel T. Muzorewa, from visiting the rural areas. However, their placards made blatant political demands beyond just the unbanning of Bishop Muzorewa. In these political campaigns Rukwadzano women drew inspiration from their Shona worldview and felt no remorse for having become "political animals." Once again, like Nehanda Nyakasikana, Chikanga, and Tekela Waponga, they were willing to put their lives on the line for the survival of their children, men, animals, environment, and community.

Thus we bring the story of Rukwadzano to the critical turning point in the 1960s and 1970s, when its hidden text began to come into the open to reveal its roots in Shona culture, searching for self-determination.

In this chapter, I showed how a group of indigenous African women through an unwritten text took the essence of the Christian gospel and fashioned and translated it into the African communal, holistic, and relational orientation to the world. I demonstrated how indigenous people, much as African Americans did, correlated the essence of Christianity with their indigenous African worldview and developed African Christianity. In short, the chapter showed that the essence of Christianity can be discerned even when the original intent of some missionaries was to Westernize Africans.

The preceding chapters demonstrated that despite the fact that colonial Christianity was patriarchal, paternalistic, racist, and culturally alienating, African women discerned the essence of the Christian message and began to take its message into their daily lives. The women in Rukwadzano fashioned faith practices similar to those found in the early church, and used its communal, holistic, and relational understanding of the world to develop a faith relevant to the lives of African people.

Moreover, these chapters showed the essential role of women in the preservation of relational, communal, and holistic values in a cultural orientation where nurturing and caring values were not sanctioned.

CHAPTER 8

Toward the Future

Tʜʀᴏᴜɢʜᴏᴜᴛ ᴛʜᴇ ʙᴏᴏᴋ, I ʜᴀᴠᴇ ᴀᴛᴛᴇᴍᴘᴛᴇᴅ ᴛᴏ sʜᴏᴡ ᴛʜᴀᴛ ᴛʜᴇ Mᴀɴʏɪᴋᴀ women and the early Methodist Episcopal Church women missionaries who first met at Old Mutare in 1900 came from two very different worlds. These differences would be reflected in Rukwadzano, which began as a Manyika women's prayer-group movement but was "tamed" into a women's church organization by the mission church.

American Protestant women missionaries came to Old Mutare after having successfully broken the nineteenth-century barriers that prevented their entry into the foreign mission field. At Old Mutare they were fellow pioneers with male missionaries in founding a Christian community among the Manyika. Even though they had come specifically assigned to work with the indigenous women, at this stage women missionaries were involved in every aspect of mission work at the center. Women missionaries went into the villages on preaching and visitation campaigns. They taught in the boys' school at the mission. Mrs. Helen Rasmussen learned the Shona language and translated the Bible.

In spite of these women's efforts for the church's ministry, the mission church, in line with its home tradition, continued to consider women's contributions marginal. Methodist Episcopal Church women missionaries came to a world where some women were demanding not just expansion of the domestic sphere but also recognition as capable and equal partners in the public arena. A volatile colonial context that deemed men's military prowess the ultimate measure of an individual's achievements also worked against the goal of these early women missionaries to be treated as equals at the mission.

Manyika women were coming from a world in which the Mutupo principle governed how individuals related to each other. Women and men, humans and animals, for the most part seemed to coexist in a harmonious environment. The British arrived in a territory teeming with wildlife and fought and hanged legendary women like Nehanda Nyakasikana who were recognized as legitimate authorities throughout Shona and Ndebele lands. This world was shattered by colonial conquest and gradually eroded by Christianization and colonization of the region.

Early women missionaries designed an education for Manyika women that barely reflected their situation and context. The education curriculum for Manyika women was primarily based on a colonial myth portraying these women as victims of a savage culture. In the process of educating women for a "Christian civilized" lifestyle, the mission church alienated Manyika woman from their land, men, and traditional communities. In Rhodesia, such a program directly advanced the colonial schemes of racist oppression and dispossession. Early women missionaries, like the church of their day, failed to acknowledge the damage and pain inflicted by racist colonialism on the women and their communities. Early indigenous women were educated and groomed simply to become wives to their husbands and mothers to their children.

However, women missionaries did equip indigenous women with the tool of literacy. As Bible women, these women were also trained to assume leadership in the newly founded Christian communities. It was with the tool of literacy that the first Manyika women at Old Mutare decided to pick up the Bible and read and exercise their own interpretation. Reading the Bible by themselves also made them realize that the world and the message of the Bible were not exactly the same as that of a "colonial Christian civilization." Drawing from the Bible and from their indigenous worldview, they started a prayer movement that met outside the mission grounds. Out of this group Rukwadzano was born.

Rukwadzano began as a Christian movement of women in search of an honest, inclusive, and affirming community. The women's vision of a church embraced all of life and they worked to sustain it. They also sought a church that acknowledged the evil of the existing racism and colonialism by challenging the system and working to heal the hurt of a land and a people. Women were seeking to build a church that healed the community and, in turn, could heal the hurt in the land. Having realized that the mission church was too absorbed in self-preservation and institution building to be self-critical, the founding mothers of Rukwadzano decided to live their vision of a church within the church. Drawing from the Manyika worldview and the Bible, these women carved a platform that gave them the opportunity to speak with authority in the colonial context and eventually in the struggle against colonialism.

In Rukwadzano, women defied the mission church's superimposed bureaucratic structure designed to choke their initiatives by turning a movement into an organization. Instead the women chose to view the structure from a Manyika perspective that regards hierarchy not in monopolistic terms but rather in terms of a relational symbiosis in the search for happiness and harmony in existence.[1] Shona women did not have to choose between an organization or a movement but successfully overcame the trap of dualism and struggled to keep an acceptable balance.[2]

A bureaucratic ecclesiastical structure failed to extinguish the zeal for mission as defined by Rukwadzano women at every level. At the organizational level they adopted and operated with the superimposed mission-church's structure of rigid hierarchy and doctrine, but at the core level women were driven by the principles of the Shona worldview that defied hierarchical as well as dictatorial forms. In Rukwadzano women created a space where, by drawing from their culture, the Bible, and experience, they constructed and sought to apply a theology of liberation for a people and land suffering great pain. In this group, women also found a community, a home, and place for healing.

Toward the Future

In an independent Zimbabwe, since they were mostly viewed as custodians of an outmoded mission church orthodoxy, Rukwadzano and similar organizations were thought to be on their way to "dying a natural death," as its mostly rural and illiterate constituency grew old and irrelevant. Instead, in the mid-1980s, women from all segments of Zimbabwean society came seeking membership in the organization.[3] The organization may not have viewed itself as having entered a new phase in its growth, but it affirmed that it had finally succeeded in communicating its message and mission of healing and liberation for women, the poor, and the environment.

In an independent Zimbabwe, women had expected their hurting to cease with the end of the colonial state. However, women gradually found themselves ignored, marginalized, and abused yet again. A major factor for this predicament was that when independence came, women lacked the qualifications needed to assume meaningful positions of power and authority. Even though women had participated at every level in the political and military struggle for independence, this book has shown that during colonialism they were neither trained nor educated to assume such positions of power. The fact that women were generally denied access to training, education, or employment during the colonial period would be a challenge for the new government.

Contemporary liberal Christianity promotes the idea that evangelical Christianity is biblically oriented in a negative way, otherworldly, politically conservative, dismissive of others who are different, and irrelevant for living life in this modern age. In fact, some dismiss the evangelistic African orientation as a creation of colonial Christianity and therefore reject its significance. However, as I have shown, it is possible for African Christians to embrace a grace-oriented, biblically based faith centered on a relationship with God through Jesus Christ that is not disengaged from this world, politically conservative, or dismissive of those who are different. Rather, this book has shown how a women's organization, through the power of the gospel, reached out to the poor and needy to lift them up and give them a sense of meaning.

Another issue emerging from the preceding chapters is that of a contemporary world in which the village is collapsing and in desperate need of recovering some of the village functions. As I pointed out, small groups are essential for living in a world that privileges individualism and treats human worth as a commodity to be bought and sold.

While this book has laid a historical foundation for the development of the Rukwadzano movement, I realize I have only scratched the surface. The implications of this movement for the ongoing struggles for justice and liberation are tremendous. Moreover, the work of this organization in the fight against the AIDS and HIV pandemic needs to be chronicled. Finally, the work of this organization and the role of women in church growth and evangelism need further exploration and documentation.

Notes

Notes to Introduction

1. Ciru Getecha and Jesimen Chipika, eds., *Zimbabwe Women's Voices* (Harare: Zimbabwe Women's Resource Center and Network, 1995).

2. Belinda Bozzoli, "Marxism, Feminism, and African Studies," *Journal of African Studies* 9 (April 1983): 2. See Shula Marks, ed., *Not Either an Experimental Doll* (Bloomington: Indiana University Press, 1987); Cherryl Walker, ed., *Women and Gender in Southern Africa* (Cape Town: David Philip & James Currey, 1990).

3. Terence O. Ranger and Isario Kimambo, *The Historical Study of African Religion* (Nairobi: Heinemann, 1972).

4. Basil Davidson, *Africa in History* (New York: Macmillan, 1991).

5. Terence O. Ranger, "Religious Movements and Politics in Sub-Saharan Africa," *African Studies Review* 29/2 (1986).

6. Hoyini K. Bhila, *Trade and Politics in a Shona Kingdom* (Harlow, United Kingdom: Longman, 1982).

7. Bishop Joseph C. Hartzell, in *Africa Diamond Jubilee Documents* (1909).

8. Interview of Mbuya Mutasa (September 9, 1992; October 15, 1993, at Seke).

9. Interview of Mbuya F. Muchirahondo Nyajeka (September 19, 1992) and Mambo A. Mutasa (September 5, 1993).

10. Aeneas S. Chigwedere, *From Mutapa to Rhodes* (London: Macmillan, 1980).

Notes to Chapter 1

1. Terence O. Ranger, *Revolt in Southern Rhodesia* (Evanston: Northwestern University Press, 1967), 301; Inus M. Daneel, *The God of the Matopo Hills* (Paris: Mouton and Co., 1970), 32; Michael Gelfand, *Medicine and Magic of the Mashona* (Cape Town: Juta, 1956); David Lan, *Guns and Rain* (Berkeley: University of California Press, 1985), 15.

2. Daneel, *The God of the Matopo Hills*, 32; Ranger, *Revolt in Southern Rhodesia*, 301.

3. *The Southern Rhodesia Native Affairs Department Annual*, 17 (1940): 3; Hoyini K. Bhila, *Trade and Politics in a Shona Kingdom* (Harlow, U.K: Longman, 1982), 241; Interview, Mambo A. Mutasa (October 8, 1993).

4. Chet Lancaster, *The Goba of the Zambezi* (Norman: University of Oklahoma Press, 1981), 195.

5. Walter Rodney, *How Europe Underdeveloped Africa* (Nairobi: Heinemann, 1972), 248; John Günther, *Inside Africa* (New York: Harper and Brothers, 1953), 295.

6. See *Heathen Woman's Friend* 11/1 (1899); Cherryl Walker, ed., *Women and Gender in Southern Africa* (Cape Town: David Philip & James Currey, 1990).

7. D. N. Beach, *The Shona and Their Neighbors* (Oxford: Blackwell, 1994), 4; A.S. Chigwedere, *From Mutapa to Rhodes: 1000 to 1890 A.D.* (London: Macmillan, 1980); Herbert Ashwanden, *Symbols of Life* (Gweru, Zimbabwe: Mambo Press, 1982), 106; *The Southern Rhodesia Native Affairs Department Annual* (1923): 7.

8. Rosemary Radford Ruether, *Gaia and God* (San Francisco: HarperCollins, 1992), 15.

9. Aeneas S. Chigwedere, *The Karanga Empire* (London: Macmillan, 1985).

10. Jay B. McDaniel, *Earth, Sky, Gods, and Mortals: Developing an Ecological Spirituality* (Mystic, Conn.: Twenty-Third Publications, 1990), 25.

11. Ibid.

12. M.F.C. Bourdillon, *The Shona Peoples: An Ethnography of the Contemporary Shona, with Special Reference to their Religion* (Gwelo, Rhodesia: Mambo Press, 1976), 34.

13. *The Southern Rhodesia Native Affairs Department Annual* (1923), 60.

14. See Victor W. Turner, *The Ritual Process* (Ithaca: Cornell University Press, 1969).

15. See James George Frazer, *The Golden Bough: A Study in Magic and Religion* (New York: The Macmillan Co., 1922), chapter 22.

16. *Southern Rhodesia Native Affairs Department Annual*, 19 (1942): 30.

17. Herbert Aschwanden, *Karanga Mythology* (Gweru, Zimbabwe: Mambo Press, 1989), 98.

18. Karen Sachs, *Sisters and Wives* (Urbana: University of Illinois Press, 1979).

19. Ranger, *Revolt in Southern Rhodesia*; Bhila, *Trade and Politics in a Shona Kingdom*.

20. A. C. Hodza, Shona *Folk Tales* (*Ngano Dzamatambidzanwa*) (Gweru, Zimbabwe: Mambo Press Lit. Bureau of Zimbabwe, 1987), 74.

Notes to Chapter 2

1. Patricia Ruth Hill, *The World Their Household* (Ann Arbor: The University of Michigan Press, 1986); Rosemary R. Ruether and Rosemary S. Keller, eds., *Women and Religion in America* (San Francisco: Harper and Row, 1981), 1: 242.

Notes

2. Helen Barrett Montgomery, *Western Women in Eastern Lands* (Norwood: Norwood Press, Cushing Berwick & Smith Co., 1910), 206; Robert Pierce Beaver, *All Love Excelling* (Grand Rapids: Eerdmans, 1968), 207.

3. *Women's Foreign Missionary Society Report*, 32 (1900-01): 192.

4. *Women's Foreign Missionary Society Report*, 33 (1903-04), 166.

5. Hoyini K. Bhila, *Trade and Politics in a Shona Kingdom* (Harlow, United Kingdom: Longman, 1982), 241.

6. Helen Springer, *Snapshots from Sunny Africa* (London: Fleming H. Revell Co., 1909), 19.

7. Rudo Gaidzanwa, *Images of Women in Zimbabwean Literature* (Harare: The College Press, 1985), 87.

8. *Conference Minutes*, Central East Africa Conference (1901).

9. Roland Oliver and Anthony Atmore, *Africa since 1800* (Cambridge: Cambridge University Press, 1982), 145; Hermann Karl W. Kumm, *African Missionary Heroes and Heroines* (New York: The McMillan Co., 1917), 119.

10. Beaver, *All Love Excelling,* 50.

11. Ibid.

12. Rosemary Radford Ruether, *Sexism and God-Talk* (Boston: Beacon Press, 1983), 242.

13. Springer, *Snapshots from Sunny Africa*, 136.

14. Ibid., 124, 133.

15. *Central East Africa Conference Minutes* (1910).

16. Ibid.

17. Ibid.

18. Ibid.

19. Janet J. Wilson, ed., *Women in American Religion* (Philadelphia: University of Pennsylvania Press, 1980), 120.

20. M. A. Sharp, *Heathen Woman's Friend*, Methodist Women's Missionary Society Journal, 11/1 (July 1879).

21. *Women's Foreign Missionary Society Report*, 32 (1900): 166.

22. Bhila, *Trade and Politics in a Shona Kingdom*, 23.

23. Hoyini Bhila, "Trade and Early Missionaries in Southern Zambezia," in *Christianity South of the Zambezi*, ed. M.F.C. Bourdillon (Gwelo, Rhodesia: Mambo Press, 1977), 2:33.

24. *Heathen Woman's Friend* 29/1 (1897):198.

25. E. H. Richards in *Central East Africa Conference Minutes* (1900).

26. Springer, *Snapshots from Sunny Africa*, 7.

27. Cecil Northcott, *Robert Moffat: Pioneer in Africa* (London: Lutterworth, 1961), 83.

28. Hartzell, *Africa Diamond Jubilee Documents*, 1909.

29. Springer, *Snapshots from Sunny Africa*, 92.

30. *Heathen Woman's Friend* 29/1 (July 1897): 198.

31. Hubert Chadwick, *Gonzalo Da Silveira* (London: Manressa Press, 1910), 67.

32. Bourdillon, *The Shona Peoples*, 1976, 68.

33. Basil Davidson, *The African Genius* (Boston: Little, Brown and Company. 1969), 60; Ernie Regehr, *Perceptions of Apartheid* (Scottdale, PA: Herald Press, 1979), 123.

34. Erwin H. Richards, *Heathen Woman's Friend* (1899), 129.

35. Wilson Thomas Hogue, *G. Harry Agnew* (Chicago: The Free Methodist Publishing House, 1886).

36. Hartzell, *Africa Diamond Jubilee Documents*, 25

37. Jean Farrant, *Mashonaland Martyr* (London: Oxford University Press, 1966), 101.

38. C.F. Andrews, *John White of Mashonaland* (London: Harper and Brothers, Publishers, 1935), 35.

39. Charlotte Crogman Wright, *Beneath the Southern Cross* (New York: Exposition Press, 1955), 123; Bourdillon, *The Shona Peoples*, 1976, 68; A. K. H. Weinrich, *African Marriage in Zimbabwe* (Gweru, Zimbabwe: Mambo Press, 1982), 43.

40. Knight George Bruce, *Memories of Mashonaland* (Bulawayo: Mardon Printers, 1887), 81.

Notes to Chapter 3

1. *Heathen Woman's Friend* (February 1870), 73.

2. *Women's Foreign Missionary Society Report*, 34 (1903-04): 177.

3. *Women's Foreign Missionary Society Report*, 36 (1904-05): 224.

4. Helen Springer, *Snapshots from Sunny Africa*, 19.

5. Hartzell, *Africa Diamond Jubilee Documents*, 46.

6. Ibid., 15.

7. *Africa News*, 11 (1889-90): 602-04.

8. Farrant, *Mashonaland Martyr*, 141; Andrews, *John White of Mashonaland*, 20.

9. Regehr, *Perceptions of Apartheid*, 118.

10. Bruce, *Memories of Mashonaland*, 98.

11. Ibid, 98, 99.

12. Farrant, *Mashonaland Martyr*, 199; Andrews, *John White of Mashonaland*, 51.

13. Hartzell, *Africa Diamond Jubilee Documents*, 25.

14. *Women's Foreign Missionary Society Report*, 32 (1899): 165.

15. Bhila, *Trade and Politics in a Shona Kingdom*, 242; Regehr, *Perceptions of Apartheid*, 119.

16. Cripps, quoted in Douglas V. Steere, *God's Irregular: Arthur Shirley Cripps* (London: SPCK Publishing, 1973), 67.

Notes

17. Ibid.

18. Andrews, *John White of Mashonaland*, 95.

19. Ibid, 20.

20. Regehr, *Perceptions of Apartheid,* 119.

21. Steere, *God's Irregular*, 125.

22. See Ruether, *Sexism and God-Talk*.

23. Rudo Gaidzanwa, *Images of Women in Zimbabwean Literature* (Harare: The College Press. Pet. Ltd., 1985).

24. *Women's Foreign Missionary Society Report*, 38 (1906): 191.

25. Mary H. Moran, *Civilized Women* (Ithaca: Cornell University Press, 1990).

26. Springer, *Snapshots from Sunny Africa*, 119.

27. Ibid, 146.

Notes to Chapter 4

1. Arthur Shearly Cripps, *An Africa for the Africans* (London: Longman's Green and Co., 1927), 142.

2. Alexander Wilmot, *Monomotapa (Rhodesia)* (London: T. P. Unwin, 1896), 158.

3. *Women's Foreign Missionary Society Report*, 35 (1902): 182.

4. Springer, *Snapshots from Sunny Africa*, 122.

5. Zelma Wood Lawyer, *I Married a Missionary* (Abilene: Christian College Press, 1943), 229.

6. Ruether, *Gaia and God*, 26-31, 173-201.

7. Herbert Aschwanden, *Symbols of Life* (Gweru, Zimbabwe: Mambo Press 1989), 106.

8. Lawrence Vambe, *An Ill-Fated People* (London: Heinemann, 1972), 6.

9. Lawyer, *I Married a Missionary*, 229.

10. Springer, *Snapshots from Sunny Africa*, 147.

11. Bruce, *Memories of Mashonaland*, 129.

12. Patricia Hill, *The World Their Household* (Ann Arbor: The University of Michigan Press, 1986), 28.

13. *Methodist Episcopal Church Conference Minutes* (1930).

14. Northcott, *Robert Moffat*, 61.

15. Lawyer, *I Married a Missionary.*

16. See Hill, *The World Their Household*; Betty Friedan, *The Feminine Mystique* (New York: Norton, 1963).

17. Jacklyn Cock, *Maids and Madams* (Johannesburg: Ravan Press, 1980), 125; Karen T. Hansen, *Distant Companions* (Ithaca: Cornell University Press, 1989), 52.

18. Lawyer, *I Married a Missionary*, 147.

19. Springer, *Snapshots from Sunny Africa*, 116.

20. *Methodist Episcopal Church Conference Minutes* (1910).

21. *Conference Minutes* (1923), 54.

22. Interview, October 5, 1993.

23. Springer, *Snapshots from Sunny Africa.*

24. Rosemary Radford Ruether and Rosemary S. Keller, eds., *Women and Religion in America* (San Francisco: Harper & Row, 1981), 1:36.

25. Mutukudzi, Album Side 1, No.3 (1978).

26. Shula Marks, ed., *Not Either an Experimental Doll* (Bloomington: Indiana University Press, 1987), 23.

Notes to Chapter 5

1. *Rumano Rwe Rukwadzano* (hereinafter *R.R.W.*, revised 1944, 1960, corrected 1974), 1.

2. Deborah Gaitskell, "Devout Domesticity: A Centory of African Women's Christianity in South Africa," in Cherryl Walker, ed., *Women and Gender in Southern Africa* (Cape Town: David Philip & James Currey, 1990), 251; Terence O. Ranger, "Connection between Primary Resistance Movements and Mass Nationalism in East and Central Africa" (East Africa Social Science Conference, 1966).

3. Terence O. Ranger and Isario Kimambo, *The Historical Study of African Religion* (Nairobi: Heimann, 1972); Wright, *Women and Gender in Southern Africa*; Adrian Hastings, *A History of African Christianity 1950-1975* (London: Cambridge University Press, 1979), 521.

4. *R.R.W.* (1974), 4, 10.

5. *Rhodesia Conference Minutes* (1928).

6. *Central East Annual Conference Minutes* (1910).

7. *R.R.W.* (1944).

8. *Methodist Episcopal Conference Minutes* (1928).

9. *The Rhodesia Missionary Advocate* (1914), 6.

10. Terence O. Ranger, *Church and State in Southern Rhodesia* (Central African History Association, 1960).

11. Allan Aubrey Boesak, *Farewell to Innocence* (Johannesburg: Ravan Press, 1976).

12. *The Rhodesia Missionary Advocate* (1913), 6.

13. Aeneas Chigwedere, *Birth of Bantu Africa* (Bulawayo, Zimbabwe: Books for Africa, 1982), 99; Steere, *God's Irregular*, 119.

14. Marc Jean Ela, *My Faith as an African* (New York: Maryknoll, 1988).

15. See Alex La Guma, *Time of the Butcherbird* (Oxford: Heinemann, 1979).

16. Gaidzanwa, *Images of Women in Zimbabwean Literature*; Tsitsi Dangarembga, *Nervous Conditions* (Seattle: The Seal Press, 1988).

17. Edward D. Alvord, "Agricultural Demonstration Work on Native Reserves." *Occasional Paper No. 3* (Department of Nature Development, 1930).

18. *Rhodesia Mission Conference Minutes* (1930).

19. C. Gates in *Methodist Episcopal Church Conference Minutes* (1930).
20. Lawrence Vambe, *An Ill-Fated People* (London: Heinemann, 1972).
21. Terence O. Ranger, *Church and State in Southern Rhodesia* (Central African History Association, 1960),
22. Hill, *The World Their Household*, 185.

Notes to Chapter 6

1. Henry Nau, *Rethinking Africa* (St. Louis: Concordia Publishing House, 1945), 23.
2. *Rhodesia Mission Conference Minutes* (1930).
3. Ibid. (1928).
4. *R.R.W.*, 4.
5. Ibid., 22.
6. Mary H. Moran, *Civilized Women* (Ithaca: Cornell University Press, 1990), 51-56.
7. *Rhodesia Mission Conference Minutes* (1929, 1930).
8. *R.R.W.*, 23.
9. Barbara Rogers, *Domestication of Women* (New York: St. Martin's Press, 1979).
10. *R.R.W.*, 24.
11. Ibid., 12, 22.
12. Ranger, *Church and State in Southern Rhodesia*.
13. *R.R.W.*, 25.
14. Ibid., 24.
15. Marks, *Not Either an Experimental Doll*, 23.
16. Vambe, *An Ill-Fated People*, 18.

Notes to Chapter 7

1. *Rhodesia Missionary Conference Minutes* (1938).
2. Filomina Chioma Steady, ed., *The Black Woman Cross-Culturally* (Cambridge: Scheinkman Publishing Company, 1981).
3. *R.R.W.*, 9.
4. Ibid.
5. Placide Tempels, *Bantu Philosophy* (Paris: Presence Africaine, 1959).
6. Friedrich Wilhelm Posselt, *Fact and Fiction: A Short Account of the Natives of Southern Rhodesia* (Bulawayo: Rhodesian Printing & Publishing Co., Ltd., 1935), 86.
7. Ibid., 88.
8. *R.R.W.*, 14, 4.
9. See Bennette Jules-Rossette, *The African Apostles* (Ithaca: Cornell University Press, 1975).

10. See Michael Gelfand, *Colonial Rule in Africa* (Madison: University of Wisconsin Press, 1979).

11. George M. Daniels, ed., *Drums of War* (New York: Joseph Okpaku Publishing Co., 1974), 137.

12. See Terence O. Ranger, *Peasant Consciousness and Guerilla War in Zimbabwe* (London: James Curry, 1985).

Notes for Chapter 8

1. Ruether, *Gaia and God*, 15; Tempels, *Bantu Philosophy* (1959).

2. Hill, *The World Their Household*, 26.

3. Ciru Getecha and Jesimen Chipika, eds., *Zimbabwe Women's Voices* (Harare: Zimbabwe Women's Resource Center and Network, 1995), 83.

Bibliography

Primary Sources

Africa News, 1889-90: Bishop William Taylor of Africa's Magazine. Location: Garrett Library Archives.

Africa Diamond Jubilee Documents (1909). Bishop Joseph C. Hartzell. Location: Garrett Library Archives.

Central East Africa Conference on Rhodesia Mission Minutes, 1900-1950. Location: Old Minute Methodist Church Archives, Zimbabwe.

Heathen Woman's Friend, 1879-1920: Methodist Women's Missionary Society Journal. Location: Garrett Library Archives.

Ngoma, 1964: *The Hymnal of the United Methodist Church in Zimbabwe*. Location: Old Mutare.

Rumano Rwe Rukwadzano (Official Handbook and Constitution), 1938; revised 1944, 1960. Location: Old Mutare Zimbabwe.

The Rhodesia Missionary Advocate, 1910-1950. Old Mutare. Location: United Methodist Church Archives.

The Southern Rhodesia Native Affairs Department Annual Report (1900-1942). Location: Northwestern University.

Women's Conference Report. Rhodesia Mission Conference (1910-1928). Location: Old Minute Methodist Church Archives, Zimbabwe.

Women's Foreign Missionary Society Report. Methodist Episcopal Church (1890-1940). Location: Garrett Library Archives

Secondary Sources

Alvord, Edward. D. "Agricultural Demonstration Work on Native Reserves." *Department of Native Development, Occasional Paper, No. 3*. Salisbury, 1930.

Andrews, C. F. *John White of Mashonaland*. London: Harper and Brothers, Publishers, 1935.

Aschwanden, Herbert. *Karanga Mythology*. Gweru: Mambo Press, 1989.

______. *Symbols of Death*. Gweru: Mambo Press, 1985.

______. *Symbols of Life*. Gweru: Mambo Press, 1982.

______. *Symbols of Life*. Gweru: Mambo Press, 1979.

Bacon, Margaret Hope. *Mothers of Feminism*. Toronto: Fitzhenry & Whiteside, 1986.

Balafamo, Tarn. *Simplified Traditional African Philosophy*. Nembe, Nigeria: Laity School of African Thought, 1978.

Banana, Canaan Sodindo. *Come and Share*. Gweru: Mambo Press, 1990.

Barrett, David B., ed. *African Initiatives in Religion*. Nairobi: East African Publishing House, 1971.

Beach, D. N. *The Shona and Their Neighbors*. Oxford: Blackwell, 1994.

Beaver, Robert Pierce. *All Love Excelling*. Grand Rapids: William B. Eerdmans Publishing Co, 1968.

Becher, Jeanne, ed. *Women, Religion and Sexuality*. Philadelphia: Trinity Press International, 1991.

Bhila, Hoyini K. *Trade and Politics in a Shona Kingdom*. Harlow, U.K: Longman, 1982.

Bingham, Marjorie Wall. *Women in Africa of the Sub-Sahara*. Hudson, Wisconsin: Gary Mccuen, 1983.

Blynden, Edward Wilmot. *African Life and Customs*. London: Phillips, 1908.

Boer, Jan Harm. *Missions: Heralds of Capitalism or Christ*. Ibadan: Day Star Press, 1984.

Boesak, Allan Aubrey. *Farewell to Innocence*. Johannesburg: Ravan Press, 1976.

_____. *Black and Reformed*. New York: Orbis Books, 1984.

Bond, George, ed. *African Christianity*. London: Academic Press, 1979.

Boone, Sylvia Ardyn. *Radiance from the Waters*. New Haven: Yale University Press, 1986.

Bourdillon, M. F. C. *Christianity South of the Zambezi*. vol. 2. Gweru: Mambo Press, 1977.

_____. *The Shona Peoples: An Ethnology of the Contemporary Shona, with Special Reference to their Religion*. Gwelo, Rhodesia: Mambo Press, 1976.

Brandel-Syrier, Mia. *Black Women in Search of God*. London: Lutterworth, 1962.

Bruce, Knight George, *Memories of Mashonaland*. Bulawayo: Mardon Printers, 1895.

Bull, Theodore, ed. Rhodesia: *Crisis of Color*. Chicago: Quadrangle Books, 1967.

Bullock, Charles. *Mashona Laws and Customs*. Salisbury: Argus Print & Publishing Co., 1913.

Calverton, V. F. ed. *Sex in Civilization*. Garden City, NY: Garden City Publishing Co., 1929.

Cason, Walter J. *The Growth of Christianity in the Liberian Environment*. Ann Arbor: University Microfilms, 1975.

Chadwick, H. *Life of the Venerable Goncalo De Silveira of the Society of Jesus*. London: Manressa Press, 1910.

Chadwick, Hubert. *Gonzalo Da Silveira*. London: Manressa Press, 1910.

Chigwedere, Aeneas. *Birth of Bantu Africa* (Bulawayo, Zimbabwe: Books for Africa, 1982)

_____. *From Mutapa to Rhodes: 1000 to 1890 A.D.* London: Macmillan, 1980.

_____. *The Karanga Empire.* London: Macmillan, 1985.

_____. *Lobola—The Pros and Cons.* Harare, Zimbabwe: Books for Africa, 1982.

_____. *From Mutapa to Rhodes.* London: Macmillan, 1980.

Christensen, T., and William R. Hutchison. *Missionary Ideologies in the Imperialist Era, 1880–1920.* Qarhus, Denmark: 1982.

Chung, Hyun Kyung. *Struggle to Be the Sun Again.* Maryknoll: Orbis, 1992.

Clark, Elizabeth Ann. *Women in the Early Church.* Wilmington: Michael Glazier, Inc., 1987.

Cochrane, James R. *Servants of Power.* Johannesburg: Ravan Press, 1987.

Cock, Jacklyn. *Maids and Madams.* Ravan Press: Johannesburg, 1980.

Comaroff, Jean. *Body of Power, Spirit of Resistance.* Chicago: University of Chicago Press, 1985.

Cripps, Arthur Shearly. *An Africa for the Africans.* London: Longmans, Green and Co. Ltd., 1927.

_____. *Chaminuka.* London: The Sheldon Press, 1928.

_____. *Lyra Evangelistica.* London: Simpkin, Marshall and Co., 1909.

Daneel, Inus M. *Zionism and Faith-Healing in Rhodesia.* Mouton: Mouton & Co., 1970.

_____. *Quest for Belonging.* Gweru: Mambo Press, 1987.

_____. *The God of the Matopo Hills.* Paris: Mouton and Co., 1970.

Daniels, George M. *Drums of War.* New York: Joseph Okpaku Publishing Co., 1974.

Dangarembga, Tsitsi. *Nervous Conditions.* Seattle: The Seal Press, 1988.

Davidson, Basil. *Africa in History.* New York: Macmillan Publishing Co., 1991.

_____. *The African Genius.* Boston: Little, Brown and Company, 1969.

_____. *Black Mother.* London: Longman, 1961.

_____. *Modern Africa,* 3rd. ed. London: Longman, 1994.

Deane, D.J. *Robert Moffatt.* London: S. W. Partridge and Co.

Delf, George. *Asians in East Africa.* London: Oxford University Press, 1963.

Dickson, Mora. *Beloved Partner.* London: Victor Gallancz Ltd., 1974.

Dinesen, Isak. *Out of Africa.* New York: Random House, 1937.

Dodge, Ralph Edward. *The Revolutionary Bishop.* Pasadena: William Carey Library, 1986.

Ela, Marc Jean. *My Faith as an African.* New York: Maryknoll, 1988.

Emmerson, Mabel E. *Mary K. Edwards.* Boston: Massachusetts Women's Board of Missions, 1917.

Exley, Richard. *The Missionary Myth.* Guildford: Lutterworth Press, 1973.

Fabella, Virginia, and Mercy Amba, Oduyoye. *With Passion and Compassion*. Maryknoll: Orbis, 1988.

Farrant, Jean. *Mashonaland Martyr*. London: Oxford University Press, 1966.

Fell, J. R. *Folk Tales of the Batonga and Other Sayings*. London: Holbom Publishing House, 1930.

Filesi, Teobaldo. *China and Africa in the Middle Ages*. London: F. Cars in association with Central Asia Research Center, 1972.

Fisher, P., ed. *The New American Studies*. Berkeley: University of California Press, 1991.

Forster, Peter G. T. *Cullen Young*. Hull, England: Hull University Press, 1989.

Fortune, George, and Mfuka, R., ed. *Ngano*. Harare: University of Zimbabwe, 1973.

Frazer, James George. *The Golden Bough: A Study in Magic and Religion*. New York: The Macmillan Co., 1922.

______. *Worship of Nature*. New York: Macmillan Co., 1926.

Freud, Sigmund. *Totem and Taboo*. New York: W. W. Norton; 1950.

Friedan, Betty. *The Feminine Mystique*. New York: Norton, 1963.

Fry, Peter. *Spirits of Protest*. Cambridge: Cambridge University Press, 1976.

Gaidzanwa, Rudo. *Images of Women in Zimbabwean Literature*. Harare: The College Press. Pet. Ltd., 1985.

Gelfand, Michael. *Colonial Rule in Africa*. Madison, Wisconsin: University of Wisconsin Press, 1979.

________. *Growing Up in a Shona Society from Birth to Marriage*. Gweru: Mambo Press, 1979.

______. *Medicine and Magic of the Mashona*. Cape Town: Juta, 1956.

______. *Mother Patrick*. Wyberg: Rustica Press Pty, 1964.

______. *Non-Racial Island of Learning*. Gweru: Mambo Press, 1979.

______. *Shona Religion, with Special Reference to the Makorekore*. Cape Town: Juta, 1962.

Getecha, Ciru, and Chipika, Jesimen, eds. *Zimbabwe Women's Voices*. Harare: Zimbabwe Women's Resource Center and Network, 1995.

Gunther, John. *Inside Africa*. New York: Harper and Brothers, 1953.

Haggard, Henry Rider. *King Solomon's Mines*. London: Cassell, 1885.

Hansen, Karen T. *Distant Companions*. Ithaca: Cornell University Press, 1989.

______. *African Encounters with Domesticity*. New Brunswick, New Jersey: Rutgers University Press, 1992.

Hansson, Gurli. *African Women and Religion*. Uppsala: Uppsala University Press, 1990.

Hastings, Adrian. *A History of African Christianity 1950–1975*. London: Cambridge University Press, 1979.

Hiebert, Paul G. *Anthropological Insights for Missionaries*. Grand Rapids,

Michigan: Baker Book House, 1985.

Hill, Patricia Ruth. *The World Their Household.* Ann Arbor: The University of Michigan Press, 1986.

Hodza, A. C. Shona *Folk Tales (Ngano Dzamatambidzanwa).* Gweru: Mambo Press Lit. Bureau of Zimbabwe, 1987.

Hogue, Wilson Thomas. *G. Harry Agnew.* Chicago: The Free Methodist Publishing House, 1905.

Hooks, Bell. *Ain't I a Woman—Black Women and Feminism.* Boston: South End Press, 1981.

Ingram, John Kells. *Outlines of the History of Religion.* Condon: A & C Black, 1900.

Jacobs, Sylvia. *Black Americans and the Missionary Movement in Africa.* Westport: Greenwood Press, 1982.

Jaffe, Hans. *A History of Africa.* London: Zed Books Ltd., 1985.

Jules-Rosette, Bennette. *The African Apostles.* Ithaca: Cornell University Press, 1975.

Karlsen, Carol F. *The Devil in the Shape of a Woman.* New York: W. W. Norton & Co., 1987.

Kast, Edith. *A Missionary Remembers.* South Africa: Wepener, 1973.

Keys, Clara Eva. *We Pioneered in Portuguese East Africa.* New York: Exposition Press, 1959.

Kringe, Ellenn, and J. Comaroff. *Essays on African Marriage in Southern Africa.* Cape Town: Juta, 1981.

Kuckertz, H. *Ancestor Religion in Southern Africa.* Cacadu, Transkei: Lumko Missiological Inst., 1981.

Kumm, Hermann Karl W. *African Missionary Heroes and Heroines.* New York: The McMullan Co., 1917

La Guma, Alex. *Time of the Butcherbird.* Oxford: Heinemann, 1979.

Lamont, Donald. S*peech from the Dock.* Essex: E.T. Heron and Co. Ltd., 1977.

Lan, David. *Guns and Rain.* Berkeley: University of California Press, 1985.

Lancaster, Chet. *The Goba of the Zambezi.* Norman: University of Oklahoma Press, 1981.

Lawyer, Zelma Wood. *I Married a Missionary.* Abilene: Christian College Press, 1943.

Lerner, Gerda. *The Creation of Patriarchy.* Oxford: University Press, 1986.

Lewis, Arthur Roland. *Rhodesia Undefeated.* Harare: Rhodesia Christian Group, 1976.

Linden, Ian. *The Catholic Church and the Struggle for Zimbabwe.* London: Longman Group Limited, 1980.

Loud, Mary F. *Minnie Clarke.* Boston: Massachusetts Women's Board of Missions, 1917.

Makhubu, Paul. *Who Are the Independent Churches?* Johannesburg:

Skotaville Publishers, 1988.

Mandela, Nelson. *The Struggle Is My Life*. New York: Pathfinder, 1986.

Marks, Shula, ed. *Not Either an Experimental Doll*. Bloomington: Indiana University Press, 1987.

Marwede, Hud H. T. *Shall Lobola Live or Die?* Cape Town: African Bookman, 1945.

Mbiti, John S. *African Religions and Philosophy*. Garden City: Doubleday and Company., 1970.

______. *Introduction to African Religion*. London: Heinemann, 1975.

McAllister, Agnes. *A Lone Woman in Africa*. New York: Hunt and Eaton, 1896.

McDaniel, Jay B. *Earth, Sky, Gods, and Mortals: Developing an Ecological Spirituality*. Mystic, Conn.: Twenty-Third Publications, 1990).

Moffatt, Robert. *Missionary Labours and Scenes in Southern Africa*. New York: Robert Carter, 1846.

Mohanty, Chandra T., ed. *Third World Women and the Politics of Feminism*. Bloomington: Indiana University Press, 1991.

Montgomery, Helen Barrett. *Western Women in Eastern Lands*. Norwood: Norwood Press; J. Cushing Berwick & Smith Co., 1910.

Moran, Mary H. *Civilized Women*. Ithaca: Cornell University Press, 1990.

Mudenge, S. I. *Christian Education at the Mutapa Court*. Harare: Zimbabwe Publishing House, 1986.

Mungoshi, Charles. *One Day Long Ago*. Harare, Zimbabwe: Baobab Books, 1991.

Nau, Henry. *Rethinking Africa*. St. Louis: Concordia Publishing House, 1945.

______. *We Move into Africa: The Planting of the Lutheran Church in Southeastern Nigeria*. St. Louis: Concordia Publishing House, 1945.

Ngubane, Harriet. *Body and Mind in Zulu Medicine*. London: University of Edinburgh, 1977.

Northcott, Cecil W. *Robert Moffat: Pioneer in Africa*. London: Lutterworth Press, 1961.

Novick, Peter. *That Noble Dream*. New York: Cambridge University Press, 1988.

Nyamiti, Charles. *The Scope of African Theology*. Kampala: Gaba Publications, 1973.

Oduyoye, Mercy Amba. *Hearing and Knowing*. Maryknoll: Orbis, 1986.

______. *The Will to Arise*. Maryknoll: Orbis, 1992.

Oliver, Caroline. *Western Women in Colonial Africa*. Westpoint: Greenwood Press, 1982.

Oliver, Roland, and Atmore Anthony. *Africa since 1800*. Cambridge: Cambridge University Press, 1982.

Oosthuizen, Gerhardus Cornelius. *Post-Christianity in Africa*. London: C. Hurst Company, 1968.

Bibliography

Palmer, Bryan D. *Descent into Discourse*. Philadelphia: Temple University Press, 1990.

Parratt, John, ed. *African Christian Theology*. London: SPCK, 1987.

Parrinder,, Edward Geoffrey, E. *African Mythology*. New York: Harper & Row, 1986.

______. *African Traditional Religion*. London: Sheldon Press, 1974.

Peires, Jeffrey B. *The Dead Will Arise*. Johannesburg: Ravan Press, 1989.

Possell, Friedrich Wilhelm. *Fact and Fiction. A Short Account of the Natives of Southern Rhodesia*. Bulawayo: Rhodesian Printing & Publishing Co., Ltd., 1935.

Quarcoopome, T. N. O. *West African Traditional Religion*. Ibadan: African University Press, 1987.

Ranger, Terence O., and Kimambo, Isario. *The Historical Study of African Religion*. Nairobi: Heimann, 1972.

Ranger, Terence O., ed. *Aspects of Central African History*. Evanston: Northwestern University Press, 1968.

______. *Church and State in Southern Rhodesia*. Central African History Association, 1960.

______. *Connection between Primary Resistance Movements and Modern Mass Nationalism in East and Central Africa*. East Africa Social Science Conference, 1966.

______. "Religious Movements and Politics in Sub-Saharan Africa." *African Studies Review* 29/2, 1986.

______. *Revolt in Southern Rhodesia*. Evanston: Northwestern University Press, 1967.

______. *Themes in the Christian History of Central Africa*. Berkeley: University Of California Press, 1975.

______. *Peasant Consciousness and Guerilla War in Zimbabwe*. London: James Curry, 1985.

Raqiya Haji Dua. *Sisters in Affliction*. London: Zed Press, 1982.

Regehr, Ernie. *Perceptions of Apartheid*. Scottdale: Herald Press, 1979.

Roberts, Andrew. *Recording East Africa's Past*. Dar es Salaam: East Africa Publishing House, 1968.

Robinson, David. *Sources of the African Past: Case Studies of Pre-Colonial African States based on Primary Materials*, 1973.

Rodney, Walter. *How Europe Underdeveloped Africa*. Nairobi: Heinemann, 1972.

Rogers, Barbara. *Domestication of Women*. New York: St. Martin's Press, 1979.

Rosaldo, Michelle Zimbalist, and Lamphere, Louise, ed. *Woman Culture and Society*. Palo Alto: Stanford University Press, 1974.

Rotberg, R. I. *Rebellion in Black Africa*. London: Oxford University Press, 1971.

Bibliography

Ruether, Rosemary Radford, and Keller, Rosemary S., ed. *Women and Religion in America*, vol. 1. San Francisco: Harper & Row, 1981.

______. *Gaia and God*. San Francisco: Harper Collins Publishing, Ltd., 1992.

______. *New Woman New Earth*. San Francisco: Harper & Row, 1975.

______. *Sexism and God-Talk*. Boston: Beacon Press, 1983.

______. *Womanguides*. Boston: Beacon Press, 1985.

Sacks, Karen. *Sisters and Wives*. Urbana: University of Illinois Press, 1979.

Samkange, Stanlake J.T. *Origins of Rhodesia*. Nairobi: Heinemann, 1968.

Scutt, Joan Frances. B*orn a Rebel*. Mbabane: Websters Ltd., 1987.

Sharp, Lesley A. *The Possessed and Dispossessed: Spirits and Identity and Power in a Madagascar Migrant Town*. Ph.D. Thesis. Ann Arbor, Michigan: University Microfilm International, 1991.

Shepperson, George. *Independent African*. Edinburgh: Edinburgh University Press, 1987.

Shewmaker, Stan. *Tonga Christianity*. South Pasadena, California: William Carm Library, 1970.

Shiva, Vandana. *Staying Alive*. London: Zed Books, 1989.

Shostak, Marjorie. Nisa: *The Life and Words of a !Kung Woman*. Cambridge: Harvard University Press, 1981.

Sibiya, Christina. *Zulu Woman: Her Autobiography*. New York: Columbia University Press, 1948.

Soga, John Henderson. *Amaxhosa*. Lovedale Press, 1931.

Springer, Helen. *Snapshots from Sunny Africa*. London: Fleming H. Revell Co., 1909.

Staunton, Irene, ed. *Mothers of the Revolution*. Bloomington: Indiana University Press, 1990.

Steady, Filomina Chioma, ed. *The Black Woman Cross-Culturally*. Cambridge: Scheinkman Publishing Company, 1981.

Steere, Douglas V. *God's Irregular: Arthur Shearly Cripps*. London: SPCK, 1973.

Sundkler, Bengt G. *Bantu Prophets in South Africa*. London: Lutterworth Press, 1948. .

Sweet, Leonard I. *The Minister's Wife*. Philadelphia: Temple University Press, 1983.

Tempels, Placide. *Bantu Philosophy*. Paris: Presence Africaine, 1959.

Temples, Placide. *Bantu Philosophy*. Antwerpen: 1946.

______. *NADA: The Southern Rhodesia Native Affairs Department Annual*. Reprinted edition. No.1 (Dec. 1923), Vol. a. (1963), No.5 (1978).

Thompson, Leonard. *A History of South Africa*. London: Yale University Press, 1990.

Thorpe, Clarence. *Zambezi Venture*. London: Cargate Press, 1960.

Turner, Victor W. *The Drums of Affliction*. Oxford: Clarendon Press, 1968.

Bibliography

______. *The Ritual Process*. Ithaca: Cornell University Press, 1969.

Vail, LeRoy, ed. *The Creation of Tribalism in Southern Africa*. Berkeley: University of California Press, 1991.

Vambe, Lawrence. *An Ill-Fated People*. London: Heinemann, 1972.

Verrier, Anthony. *The Road to Zimbabwe. 1890–1980*. London: J. Cape Pub., 1986.

Villa-Vicencio, Charles. *Trapped in Apartheid*. Maryknoll: Orbis Books, 1988.

Vischer, Lukas, ed. *The History of the Church in the Third World*. Geneva: EATWO, 1983.

Von Hoffman, Carl. *Jungle Gods*. New York: H. Holt & Co., 1929.

Walker, Cherryl, ed. *Women and Gender in Southern Africa*. Cape Town: David Philip & James Currey, 1990.

Weinrich, A. K. H. *African Marriage in Zimbabwe*. Gweru: Mambo Press, 1982.

Weiss, Ruth. *The Women of Zimbabwe*. London: Kestro Publications, 1986.

Whisson, M. G. *Religion and Social Change in Southern Africa*. Cape Town: David Philip, 1975.

White, Landeg. Magomero: *Portrait of an African Village*. Cambridge: Cambridge University Press, 1987.

Williams, Walker. *Black Americans and the Evangelization of Africa*. London: University of Wisconsin Press, 1982.

Willoughby, William C. *The Soul of the Bantu*. Garden City: Doubleday, Doran & Co., 1928.

Wilmot, Alexander. *Monomotapa (Rhodesia)*. London: T.P. Unwin, 1896.

Wilson, Janet J., ed. *Women in American Religion*. University of Pennsylvania Press, 1980.

Wright, Charlotte Crogman. *Beneath the Southern Cross*. New York: Exposition Press, 1955.

Yon, D.A., Ed. *Sources and Perspectives: Aspects of Zimbabwe History Pre-Colonial to 1948*. Harare: Ministry of Education and Culture, 1990.

Young, Josiah. *Black and African Theologies*. Maryknoll: Orbis, 1986.

________. *Lumpa Church: The Lenshina Movement in Northern Rhodesia*. The Catholic General Secretariat. Xerographic Copy, 1960.

CPSIA information can be obtained at www.ICGtesting.com
Printed in the USA
LVOW081941210513

334869LV00002B/515/A